Framework FOCUS

EXERCISE BANK

8 = 0.1 = $\frac{1}{3}$

Numbers and the Number System

Dr Sue Waring

Published by Letts Educational
The Chiswick Centre
414 Chiswick High Road
London W4 5TF
tel: 020 8996 3333
fax: 020 8742 8390
email: mail@lettsed.co.uk
website: www.letts-education.com

Letts Educational is part of the Granada Learning Group. Granada Learning is a
division of Granada plc.

First published 2003

ISBN 1 84085 8834

British Library Cataloguing in Publication Data

A catalogue record for this book is available from the British Library.

Commissioned by Helen Clark

Project management by Vicky Butt

Cover design by bigtop, Bicester, UK

Editorial, layout and illustration by Hart McLeod, Cambridge

Production by PDQ

Printed and bound by Canale, Italy

Contents

Objectives are numbered consecutively within each topic as laid out in the Mathematics Framework, pages 6–11. Objectives listed in bold type are Key Objectives.
N = Numbers and the number system   C = Calculations

YEAR 9

Objectives are numbered consecutively within each topic as laid out in the Mathematics Framework, pages 6–11. Objectives listed in bold type are Key Objectives. Objectives in italic are listed in the Framework as containing material suitable for more able students.
N = Numbers and the number system   C = Calculations

~

The Letts *Exercise Bank* series has been written specifically to match the Framework for Teaching Mathematics. Each book contains exercises focused on a particular Framework topic, and can be used alongside any course or Scheme of Work.

The book is clearly divided into work for Years 7, 8 and 9. Each unit contains Essential Exercises, Consolidation Exercises and Challenging Exercises.

Throughout this book you will see the following symbols:

  This indicates a 'self test' question. Pupils can check their understanding of each unit by using the answers provided at the back of the book (page 111).

    This indicates that a calculator is required.

    Problem-solving questions are indicated by this symbol.

    Questions featuring this symbol are suggested as homework.

PLACE VALUE IN INTEGERS

Essential Exercises

1 Write in figures:

   a   two million and four

   b   twenty million five hundred

2 Write in words:

   a   4 000 060   **b**   8 000 700   **c**   300 003

3 Increase the hundreds digit of 632 508 by seven.

4 Add forty thousand to a million. Write the answer in figures.

5 Increase 999 998 by 5.

6 Calculate:

   a 40×30 **b** $1\,380\,000 \div 1000$

   c   ✓ 200×700 **d** $140\,000 \times 300$

   e $45\,000 \div 5$ **f** $109\,000 \div 100$

   g   ✓ $360\,000 \div 90$ **h** $46\,000 \div 200$

7 Write down the value, in words and then in figures, of the underlined digit in these numbers.

   a   23 0<u>6</u>1 749   **b**   4<u>5</u> 008 367   **c**   ✓ 10 <u>7</u>40 362

8 Find the sum of five hundred and nine and one thousand and twenty one. Write the answer in figures.

9 A giant box of 'Choccos' contains 200 chocolates. How many chocolates are there in 80 boxes?

10 A book case has six shelves each 2 metres long. How many centimetres of shelving is this?

Consolidation Exercises

11 🏠 What are the next two numbers in these sequences?

a 1950, 1970, 1990, ... , ...

b 22 000 007, 24 000 007, 26 000 007, ... , ...

12 Increase each of these numbers by five thousand. Write your answer in both words and figures.

a eleven million eleven thousand and eleven

b fifty million and fifty

13 What is the difference between the values of the fours in the number 24 964?

14 Change 8 kilometres into millimetres.

15 Work out:

a 29 000 × 500

b ✓ 620 × 4000

c 3 500 ÷ 70

d ✓ 2 424 000 ÷ 40

e (2002 + 220) × 3

f (400 000 + 4 000) ÷ 2000

Challenging Exercises

16 Find the difference between two million and four, and four million and two.

17 What are the next two numbers in this sequence?

1401, 2001, 2601, ... , ...

18 🏠 What is the rule for continuing these sequences?

a 10 002, 9997, 9992, ... , ...

b 22 222 222, 24 222 522, 26 222 822, ... , ...

19 Decrease ten million by ten.

20 What is the difference between the values of the odd digits in the number 5692 ?

PLACE VALUE IN DECIMALS

Essential Exercises

1 Write down:
  a the hundredths digit in 5.361
  b the thousandths digit in 2.076

2 Write as a decimal the following numbers:
  a seven and forty three hundredths
  b seven thousand and thirty four thousandths.

3 Calculate:
  a 3.8×10 **b** ✓ 4.05×100 **c** $450 \div 100$ **d** ✓ $24 \div 100$

4 Write in words:
  a 26.502   **b** 3.064   **c** £102.86   **d** £7.08
  e Find the difference between the values of the eights in **c** and **d**.

5 Write down the value of the underlined digits in these numbers:
  a 7.9<u>3</u>2   **b** 26.<u>9</u>27   **c** 153.72<u>9</u>   **d** ✓ 42.0<u>5</u>2

6 Calculate:
  a $3.57 + 0.4$ **b** $3.57 + 0.09$ **c** $3.57 - 0.03$

7 Write down the missing numbers or digits with a helpful calculation. The first one is done for you.

In this number	change this digit	like this	using this calculation	to give new number
2.58	tenths	+4	2.58 + 0.4	2.98
a 7.861	tenths	−7	_____	_____
b 23.756	thousandths	+8	_____	_____
c 0.519	_____	+3	_____	0.549
d 18.042	_____	_____	_____	18.542
e 2.163	hundredths	−9	_____	_____

8 A magazine costs £1.05. What is the cost of 20 of the magazines?

1
+
8
10,000
÷
2/3
×
+
8
43
÷
1
10,000
×
1
4
9
16

9 Work out: **a** $10.73 + 0.8$ **b** ✓ $10.73 + 0.09$.

10 Work out: **a** $7.528 - 0.03$ **b** ✓ $7.528 - 0.009$.

11 Calculate:
    a 23.74×10 **b** 2.518×1000 **c** ✓ $237.1 \div 100$ **d** $7.4 \div 10$

12 Add seventeen hundredths to 6.75.

13 How many hundredths are there altogether in the number twelve point six two?

14 🏠 Work out:
    a $(20\,000 + 400) \times 2$ **b** 800^2 **c** $(500\,000 - 80\,000) \div (300 - 90)$

Challenging Exercises

15 When one of the digits in the number 40.861 is decreased by 9 the new number is 40.771. Write down the original value of the changed digit.

16 Calculate:
    a 0.027×100 **b** 67.2×1000 **c** $64.7 \div 100$
    d $2.5 \div 1000$ **e** $0.064 \div 10$ **f** $4\,584.2 \div 100\,000$

17 A number was multiplied by 1000. The answer was 26.1. What was the number?

18 🏠 Find the difference between the values of the twos in the number 128.725.

19 Find the number which is:
    a 0.1 less than 6.0   **b** 0.01 less than 2.40

WRITTEN CALCULATIONS

Essential Exercises

Calculate these. When you have finished each question check your answers first without, and then with a calculator.

1 ✓ **a**
```
    358
     59
+ 2 497
_____
```
b
```
  49 605
   3 841
     692
+ 29 053
_____
```

2 ✓ **a**
```
  5 307
− 2 824
_____
```
b
```
  36 536
−  8 408
_____
```

3 ✓ **a**
```
   382
×   17
____
```
b
```
   752
×   31
____
```

4 ✓ **a** 17)‾901‾   **b** 23)‾897‾

5 **a**
```
  372.51
   53.37
+ 824.65
_____
```
b
```
  204.83
    7.94
  561.68
+  47.02
_____
```

6 **a**
```
  842.38
− 267.52
_____
```
b
```
  2 751.8
−  939.43
_____
```

7 **a**
```
   38.9
×    7
____
```
b
```
  237.25
×      6
_____
```

8 **a** 9)‾147.6‾   **b** 5)‾361.85‾

Consolidation Exercises

Calculate these. When you have finished each question check your answers first without, and then with a calculator.

9 a Add 382, 73, 105 and 5206.
   b Find the total of 302 961, 76 348 and 9004.

10 a Subtract 89 from 2517.
   b Find the difference between 40 651 and 9253.

11 a Multiply 705 by 24.
   b Find the product of 481 and 27.

12 a Find 798 ÷ 19.
   b Find the remainder when 750 is divided by 13.

13 a Find the sum of 5.83, 27.4 and 60.52.
   b Find the total of 204.52, 50.9 and 473.06.

14 a Take 45.72 from 183.28.
   b Find the difference between 97.26 and 63.78.

15 a Find the product of 23.58 and 9.
   b Multiply 483.72 by 8.

16 a Divide 98.56 by 8.
   b Find 512.68 ÷ 7.

17 Take 6.417 from the sum of 23.7, 48 and 151.43.

18 Multiply the total of 298, 170.9 and 2.463, by 6.

19 a Find the sum of 4.286 and 2.714.
   b Find the difference between 34.68 and 19.075.
   c Find the product of your answers.

20 Find the average of 23.54, 20.7, 19.08 and 18.36.

ORDERING DECIMALS

Essential Exercises

1 Write this list in order starting with the smallest amount: 217p, £12.70, £1.27.

2 Which one of these is less than 0.4 m: 40 cm, 400 mm, 40 mm, 400 cm?

3 Which is the shorter in each pair?
   a 2.483 km or 2.48 km   **b** ✓ 34 mm or 3.6 cm

4 Which is the heavier in each pair?
   a 3.74 kg or 3.47 kg   **b** 2400 g or 2.5 kg

5 Write down **a** the lightest and **b** the heaviest in this set: 7 kg, 700 g, 0.75 kg.

6 Write these lists in order, starting with the smallest.
   a 7.5 m, 7.3 m, 7.58 m   **b** ✓ 3.24 g, 3.39 g, 3.3 g   **c** £6.92, £6.29, £7

7 Convert these measurements into millimetres and list them
in order, with the smallest first.   3250 mm, 3.1 m, 37.9 cm, 3.473 m

8 Write down the numbers indicated by the arrows on this number line.

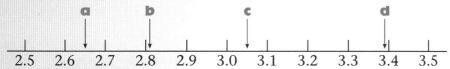

9 Draw a number line like the one in question **8** from 7.2 to 8.2 and indicate
the following numbers with an arrow.   7.55, 8.05, 7.92, 8.16

10 Write down the numbers indicated by the arrows on this number line

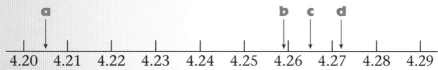

11 Write down the next three terms of these sequences.
   a 6.5, 6.6, 6.7, 6.8, ..., ..., ...   **b** 3.25, 3.24, 3.23, 3.22, ..., ..., ...

12 Find the number halfway between
   a 8.3 and 8.7
   b 2.74 and 2.78

13 Copy and complete these statements with a decimal number.
   a 6.4 is halfway between 6.2 and …
   b 3.9 is halfway between 3.6 and … .

14 Use >, <, or = to compare 0.07 with the following numbers:
   a 0.69
   b 0.008
   c 0.070
   d 0.069

15 Copy these pairs of numbers and put <, >, or = between them.
   a 7.09 7.2 **b** 3.4 3.008 **c** 0.6 0.600 **d** $\frac{3}{100}$ 0.004

16 A curtain rail is to be fitted over a window 190 cm wide and must extend 0.1 m either side of the edge of the window. Is a rail of length 2.2 m long enough? Explain.

17 A room is 3.83 m long. How many centimetres less than 4 m is this?

18 A button measures 1.24 cm across (its diameter). Will it fit through a buttonhole 0.012 m long? Explain your answer.

Consolidation Exercises

19 Which is the heavier in each of these pairs:
   a 8.6 kg or 8550 g
   b 4650 g or 4.56 kg?

20 Copy these and put > or < between them.
   a 2.68 m 270 cm
   b £650 6900p
   c 4.26 kg 4.253 kg

21 Write these lists in order starting with the largest.
   a 7.85 cm, 8.75 cm, 7.57cm
   b 3.2 kg, 3.19 kg, 3.27 kg
   c 0.12 m, 0.21 m, 25 cm

22 Find a length with 1 decimal place which is between:
   a 9.7 m and 9.5 m
   b 8.64 m and 8.72 m
   c 5.364 km and 5.472 km.

23 Which is greater: 0.499 m or 490 mm?

24 🏠 Write down the next three terms of these sequences:
- **a** 0.43, 0.45, 0,47, 0.49, …, …, …
- **b** 22.5, 22.0, 21.5, 21.0, …, …, …

25 Find the number halfway between:
- **a** 5.97 and 6.05
- **b** ✓ 7.232 and 7.244

26 ✓ Write down **a** the longest and **b** shortest in this set of lengths.

21 mm, 0.25 m, 23 cm, 2.3 cm

27 Find the difference between the lightest and heaviest in this list.

245 g, 2.45 kg, 0.425 kg, 0.25 kg

28 💡 A birthday card is 153 mm wide. Will it fit into an envelope 15 cm wide? Explain your answer.

Challenging Exercises

29 Find three equal pairs of lengths from this set. Which is the odd one out?

0.45 km, 0.045 m, 0.45 m, 4.5 cm, 45 000 cm, 450 cm, 450 mm

30 List these weights in increasing order: 7500 g, 7.8 kg, 80 000 mg, 7.08 kg.

31 Copy these and put > or < or = between them.
- **a** 3.09 cm 31 mm
- **b** 0.905 km 905 m
- **c** 64 g 0.46 kg

32 Find a weight with 1 decimal place which is between:
- **a** 0.362 g and 0.426 g
- **b** 2.863 kg and 2.985 kg.

33 Find a distance with 2 decimal places which is between:
- **a** 4.532 km and 4.546 km
- **b** 8.365 km and 8.356 km.

34 🏠 Find the sum of the smallest and largest numbers in this set.

40.208, 42.028, 40.280, 48.204, 42.820, 40.080, 48.042

35 Which is bigger: 0.467 ÷ 100 or 0.000 476 × 10?

36 Write down the next three terms in this sequence: 8.4, 8.35, 8.3, …, …, …

7 ROUNDING INTEGERS

1 Round 137 cm to: **a** the nearest metre **b** the nearest 10 cm.

2 ✓ Round 1875 g to:
 a the nearest kg **b** the nearest 100 g **c** the nearest 10 g.

3 Round these numbers to the nearest 10. 23 67 234 708 6428

4 Round these numbers to the nearest 100. 763 521 609 2691 24 608

5 Round these numbers to the nearest 1000.
 8377 7959 4296 2648 847 421

6 ✓ A number is 230 when it is rounded to the nearest 10.
 a What is the least it could be?
 b What is the most it could be?

7 A number is 860 when it is rounded to the nearest 10.
 a What is the least it could be?
 b What is the most it could be?

8 A number is 400 when it is rounded to the nearest 10.
 a What is the least it could be?
 b What is the most it could be?

9 **a** Round 41 and 73 to the nearest 10.
 b Use your answer to **a** to find a rough value for 41×73.

10 The label on a packet of biscuits says that it contains 3438 units of energy. Round this figure to the nearest hundred.

11 To the nearest 10 there are 40 sweets in a bag. What is the least and greatest number of sweets in the bag?

1 + 8 10,000 ÷ 2/3 × + 8 43 ÷ 1 10,000 × 1 4 9 16

Consolidation Exercises

12 Round the following numbers to the nearest 10 and estimate the answers to these calculations:

    a ✓ 23×74 **b** 47×52 **c** 89×41 **d** 75×38

13 Calculate the exact answers for question **12**.

14 🏠 Round the following numbers to the nearest 100 and estimate the answers to these calculations.

    a 378×241 **b** 654×298 **c** 450×109

15 A number is 700 rounded to the nearest hundred. Find the difference between the least and the most it could be.

16 🔅 Eight pupils can sit at each table in the school dining hall. How many tables are needed for 165 pupils?

Challenging Exercises

17 Round 4998 to the nearest: **a** 10   **b** 100   **c** 1000

18 Round the following numbers to the nearest 10 and estimate the answers to these calculations.

    a $241 \div 39$ **b** $719 \div 85$ **c** $207 \div 69$

19 🏠 Round the following numbers to one significant figure (1 s.f.) and estimate the answers to these calculations.

    a 71×295 **b** 3860×308 **c** 7841×95
    d 3505×46 **e** $7842 \div 197$

20 Estimate the value of $(297 + 501) \times 39$ to 1 s.f.

7 ROUNDING DECIMALS

1 Round 34.76 cm to:
  a the nearest centimetre
  b one decimal place (d.p.).

2 Round 24.38 kg to: **a** the nearest kilogram **b** 1 d.p.

3 Round 8.19 litres to: **a** the nearest litre **b** 1 d.p.

4 ✓ Round 62.96 m to: **a** the nearest metre **b** 1 d.p.

5 Round 55.55 kg to: **a** the nearest kilogram **b** 1 d.p.

6 Round 79.99 cm to: **a** the nearest centimetre **b** 1 d.p.

7 Round these numbers to the nearest whole number.
  a 6.72 **b** 2.31 **c** ✓ 4.39 **d** 9.53

8 Round these numbers to 1 d.p.
  a 3.69 **b** 8.31 **c** ✓ 7.05 **d** 7.98

9 **a** Round 4.9 and 7.1 to the nearest whole number (integer).
  b Use your answers to **a** to find a rough value for 4.9 × 7.1.

10 A shelf is 1.2 m long when measured to 1 d.p. What is the shortest length the shelf could be?

11 A parcel weighs 3.4 kg when measured to 1 d.p. What is the most it could weigh?

12 A picture is 12.5 cm wide and 22.7 cm long measured correct to 1 d.p. What is the narrowest and shortest the picture could be?

Consolidation Exercises

13 a ✓ Round 5.92 and 3.09 to the nearest whole number (integer).
  b Use your answers to **a** to find a rough value for 5.92×3.09.

14 a Round 2.31, 6.94 and 3.17 to the nearest whole number (integer).
  b Use your answers to **a** to find a rough value for $2.31 \times (6.94 + 3.17)$.

15 🏠 Estimate the answers to the following calculations by rounding each number to the nearest integer:
  a 5.1×3.7 **b** 7.5×8.2 **c** $(4.7 + 6.2) \times 1.9$ **d** $27.9 \div 4.2$

16 A number with one decimal place is 8 when rounded to the nearest integer. What is the least the number could be?

17 A number with two decimal places is 7.4 when rounded to one decimal place. What is the least the number could be?

Challenging Exercises

18 Round 39.09 to: **a** 1 d.p.   **b** 1 significant figure.
  c Find the difference between your answers to **a** and **b**.

19 Estimate the answers to the following calculations by rounding each number to the nearest integer:
  a 3.72×8.19 **b** $65.81 \div 3.09$ **c** $2.15 \times 6.08 \times 4.17$

20 Round your answers to question **19** to one significant figure.

21 🏠 Round the following numbers to 1 s.f. and estimate the answers to these calculations:
  a 2.49×23.98 **b** 56.34×7.09 **c** $81.99 \div 16.66$

7 NEGATIVE NUMBERS

Essential Exercises

1 Copy this number line and put in the missing numbers.

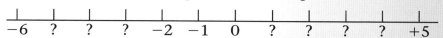

−6 ? ? ? −2 −1 0 ? ? ? ? +5

2 Draw similar number lines and label them with the following numbers.

a from −3 to +8   b from −6 to +3

c from −1 to +7   d from −4 to +2

3 Draw a thermometer labelled from −15°C to 25°C and show these temperatures on it:

> 15°C   −4°C   −10°C   20°C   −8°C

4 Find the final positions of these objects:

a start at −5 and move forward 9

b ✓ start at 3 and move backwards 7

c ✓ start at −2 and move backwards 3

d start at −7 and move forwards 5.

5 For each of these moves write down an appropriate integer:

a from +8 to +5   b ✓ from −3 to +2

c from +6 to −1   d from −7 to −4.

6 Here is a set of cards.

What are the scores for the following selections of cards?

a −1, +2, −1, 0, +2, −1, −1, 0, 0, −1

b Six cards with −1, two with +2 and one with 0.

7 a Which is higher, a temperature of +3°C or −8°C?

b The temperature fell by 7°C from 3°C. What was the new temperature?

c The temperature rose by 10°C from −4°C. What was the new temperature?

You may find a number line labelled from −10 to +10 helpful for these questions.

8 Write down the larger number from each of these pairs.
   a −1 and +7
   b +6 and −8

9 Write down the smaller number from each of these pairs.
   a +2 and −4
   b +6 and −6

10 Write these sets of numbers in order starting with the smallest.
   a 4, −2, 9, −7, 0
   b 5, −9, −14, 25, 0, −2, 16

11 Write these sets of numbers in order starting with the largest.
   a 1, −4, −8, 5, 0, −3
   b 10, −15, 13, −8, −1, 4, 21

12 What number is:
   a one less than −4
   b two more than −7
   c 5 more than −1?

You may find a number line helpful for these questions.

13 Write > or < between these pairs of numbers.
   a −5   +3
   b −1   −7
   c −3   +20

14 Write down the number halfway between these pairs.
   a ✓ −4 and +8
   b +7 and −7
   c −5 and +19
   d −11 and +13
   e −20 and +10
   f −50 and −30

15 Write down a positive or negative number for each of these situations.
   a Sportswear is on the fourth floor.
   b A scuba diver is 5 m below sea level.
   c A win in a raffle of £25.
   d A rabbit in a burrow 2 m below ground.
   e A debt of £10.

16 A lift started at the second floor and stopped at the first floor below the ground floor. How many floors did it go down? Write down an appropriate integer.

17 The sum of two numbers was 5. One of the numbers was 9. What was the other?

18 Find the final positions of these objects.

   a ✓ | Start at −2. | Move forward 5 units. | Move backwards 3 units.

   b | Start at 4. | Move backwards 7 units. | Move forward 2 units.

   c Start at −6. | Move forward 10 units. | Move backwards 8 units.

   d | Start at 3. | Move backwards 5 units. | Move backwards 4 units.

19 🏠 Find the final positions of these objects.

   a | Start at −10. | Move forward 7 units. | Move backwards 3 units.

   b | Start at 14. | Move backwards 17 units. | Move forward 3 units.

   c | Start at 8. | Move backwards 11 units twice.

20 Show the following sets of numbers on a number line.

   a from −10 to +6 in twos   **b** between −40 and +30 in tens

21 Here is a set of cards.

   −2   −1   0   +1   +2

What are the scores for the following selections of cards?

   a −2, +2, −1, 0, +1, −2, −1, 0, 0, −1

   b Three cards with +1, two with 0, four with −2 and five with −1.

   c Five cards with −2, two with +1, three with +2 and one with 0.

22 Find the mean of these temperatures.   3°C   −5°C   7°C   −1°C

23 ✓ Ann's height is 132 cm to the nearest centimetre. Copy and complete this statement about her height:

   Ann's height is 132 ± ☐ cm

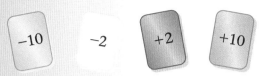

24 Here is a set of cards.

-10 -2 $+2$ $+10$

What are the scores for the following selections of cards?

a $+10$, -2, -2, -10, $+2$, $+10$

b One card with $+10$, three cards with -2, and one with -10.

c Two cards with $+10$, ten with -2, one with -10 and four with $+2$.

25 Write down the next four terms of these patterns:

a $+10$, $+8$, $+6$, $+4$, ..., ..., ..., ...

b -16, -14, -12, -10, ..., ..., ..., ...

c $+25$, $+20$, $+15$, $+10$, ..., ..., ..., ...

26 🏠 Copy and complete this table which shows positions and moves along a number line.

	Start	Move	End
a	-3	forward 12	...
b	-4	...	4
c	...	backwards 3	-5
d	-6	...	-2
e	$+3$	down 10	...
f	-10	up 40	...
g	$+5$	...	-15
h	...	forward 10	-20

27 💡 Play *Snakes and Ladders* and list any moves up ladders or down snakes with appropriate integers.

1 + 8 10,000 ÷ 2/3 × + 8 43 ÷ 1 10,000 × 1 4 9 16

MULTIPLES, FACTORS AND PRIME NUMBERS

Essential Exercises

1 Write down whether the following statements are true or false.
  a 2 is the only even prime number
  b 2 is the second prime number
  c 1 is a prime number
  d There are two prime numbers between 20 and 30.
  e A prime number has no factors.
  f There are five prime numbers less than 10.
  g The first prime number greater than 40 is 41.

2 List the first five prime numbers greater than 10.

3 Which of these is not prime? 7, 17, 27, 37, 47

4 **a** ✓ List the multiples of 9 between 50 and 100.
  b List the first six multiples of 6 greater than 50.

5 **a** What is the 9th multiple of 7? **b** What is the 8th multiple of 11?

6 Six is a factor of three of the following numbers. List them.
  26, 30, 34, 39, 42, 54, 58

7 Write down all the factors of:
  a 18   **b** ✓ 28   **c** 45   **d** 132   **e** 200

8 Find as many common factors as you can for each of these sets of numbers.
  a 8, 24, 32, 48   **b** 6, 12, 30, 36

9 **a** Which of these has a factor of 4? 28, 38, 52, 58, 62, 72

  b Which of these is a multiple of 3? 31, 41, 51, 71, 81

  c Which of these can be divided exactly by 2 and by 5?
    22, 35, 40, 52, 55, 70

  d Which of these is divisible by 9? 43, 63, 74, 81, 89, 96

10 a List all the multiples of 8 less than 50.
  b List all the multiples of 6 less than 50.
  c What is the lowest common multiple (LCM) of 6 and 8?

11 a ✓ List multiples of 2 and 5 up to 20 to find the LCM of 2 and 5.
  b List multiples of 4 and 10 up to 40 to find the LCM of 4 and 10.

12 a List all the factors of 30.
  b List all the factors of 42.
  c What is the highest common factor (HCF) of 30 and 42?

13 Repeat question **12** to find the HCF of these pairs:
  a ✓ 10 and 15   **b** 24 and 56

14 🏠 Write down whether the following statements are true or false.
  a 6 is a divisor of 36   **b** only numbers ending in 5 are divisible by 5
  c 18 is divisible by 8   **d** 2 is a common factor of all even numbers
  e 40 is the LCM of 8 and 20   **f** 6 is the HCF of 36 and 48
  g 30 has five factors less than 10
  h 12 is the largest factor of 60.

15 🔆 What is the smallest number of sweets that can be shared equally amongst 3 or 4 or 8 children?

Consolidation Exercises

16 12 has three different pairs of factors:

  | 1 × 12 (or 12 × 1) | 2 × 6 (or 6 × 2) | 3 × 4 (or 4 × 3) |

  Find all the pairs of factors of: **a** 20   **b** 32   **c** 44

17 Which of these is divisible by 9: 117, 135, 161, 226, 396?

18 What is the next multiple of 16 after 160?

1
+
8
10,000
÷
2/3
×
+
8
43
÷
1
10,000
×
1
4
9
16

19 For the set of numbers 21, 28, 42, 51, 54, 56, 66, 84:
  a list those which are divisible by 2
  b list those which are divisible by 3.
  c Explain how your answers to **a** and **b** can be used to find which of these numbers is divisible by 6.

20 Find the LCM of:
  a 9 and 12   **b** ✓ 8 and 10   **c** 15 and 20   **d** 16 and 40

21 Find the HCF of:
  a 24 and 30   **b** ✓ 36 and 54   **c** 32 and 56   **d** 18, 30 and 42

Challenging Exercises

22 True or false? Explain your answers.
  a 2 is the only prime factor of 8   **b** the prime numbers less than 10 sum to 18
  c 12 is not a multiple of 24   **d** 30 has more factors than 32

23 24 can be factorised in six different ways (excluding using 1):

   2×12 3×8 4×6 $2 \times 2 \times 6$ $2 \times 3 \times 4$ $2 \times 2 \times 2 \times 3$

  Factorise the following numbers in as many different ways as you can.
  a 20   **b** 45   **c** 100

24 Show how to use factors to work out some products mentally. For example:

   $45 \times 14 = 9 \times 5 \times 2 \times 7 = 9 \times 10 \times 7 = 90 \times 7 = 630$

  a 55×8 **b** 16×25 **c** 75×12

25 Use the clues to find these two numbers.
  a It is less than 200 but nearer to 200 than 100. It is divisible by 2, 3 and 5.
  b It is between 150 and 180. It is not divisible by a prime number less than 10. It has exactly three factors.

26 What is the HCF of: **a** 18, 30 and 42   **b** 20, 40 and 100?

27 🏠 What is the LCM of: **a** 4, 5 and 6   **b** 20, 30 and 40?

SOME SPECIAL NUMBERS

Essential Exercises

1 Find the fifth square number.

2 What is 7^2?

3 Which of these numbers is a square number: 16, 21, 36, 64, 71, 81?

4 What is the first square number greater than 50?

5 Write down the square root of: **a** 100   **b** 4   **c** 36

6 Find: **a** $\sqrt{9}$ **b** ✓ $\sqrt{49}$ **c** $\sqrt{121}$

7 Write down the first six triangular numbers.

8 ✓ Add 3^2 and 4^2.

9 Find $5^2 + 10^2$.

Consolidation Exercises

10 🏠 Find the sum of the first five square numbers.

11 Double the sixth square number.

12 Find: **a** ✓ 20^2 **b** 50^2 **c** 100^2

13 What is the difference between the fifth triangular number and the fourth square number?

14 🖩 Use your calculator to find:

   a ✓ $\sqrt{30}$ correct to 1 decimal place   **b** $\sqrt{58}$ correct to 1 d.p.?

15 Find the square root of $3^2 + 4^2$.

Challenging Exercises

16 🏠 Work out:

   a $(5^2 + 7^2) \times 2$ **b** $10 \times 3^2 + 4^2$ **c** $9^2 - 3 \times 5^2$

17 Find the square roots of the following numbers:

   a 400   **b** 6400   **c** 90 000

18 **a** $\sqrt{40}$ lies between two consecutive integers. What are they?

   b 🖩 Use your calculator to find $\sqrt{40}$ correct to 1 decimal place.

1 + 8 10,000 ÷ 2/3 × + 8 43 ÷ 1 10,000 × 1 4 9 16

FRACTIONS

1 What fraction of these shapes is shaded?

2 This diagram shows $\frac{2}{5}$ of a line of length 10 cm.

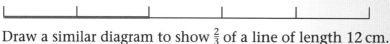

Draw a similar diagram to show $\frac{2}{3}$ of a line of length 12 cm.

3 Copy these shapes and divide each of them into eighths. Shade $\frac{5}{8}$ blue.

4 a Copy and shade $\frac{1}{3}$ of this shape. **b** Copy and shade $\frac{2}{6}$ of this rectangle.

c Copy and complete this sentence:

$\frac{1}{3}$ and $\frac{2}{6}$ are called .... fractions because they have equal values.

5 For each of these diagrams:

 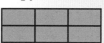

$\frac{5}{15}$ $\frac{7}{14}$ $\frac{3}{12}$

a copy the rectangle and shade the fraction written underneath
b write down an equivalent fraction with numerator 1.

6 Bags of potatoes are sold in two sizes, 2 kg and 5 kg.
What fraction is the smaller bag compared to the larger bag?

1
+
8
10,000 ÷
2/3
×
+
8
43
÷
1
10,000
×
1
4
9
16

7 Write the first quantity as a fraction of the second.
- **a** ✓ £5, £8
- **b** 25 cm, 1 m
- **c** 120°, 360°

8 What fraction is 7 mm of 1 cm?

9 Find the missing numerators.
- **a** $\frac{2}{5} = \frac{\blacksquare}{15}$
- **b** $\frac{1}{2} = \frac{\blacksquare}{12}$
- **c** ✓ $\frac{2}{3} = \frac{\blacksquare}{9}$
- **d** $\frac{4}{7} = \frac{\blacksquare}{70}$

10 Find the missing denominators.
- **a** $\frac{18}{24} = \frac{3}{\blacksquare}$
- **b** $\frac{20}{25} = \frac{4}{\blacksquare}$
- **c** ✓ $\frac{3}{7} = \frac{9}{\blacksquare}$
- **d** $\frac{5}{9} = \frac{50}{\blacksquare}$

11 Copy and complete the following:
- **a** $\frac{8}{12} = \frac{\blacksquare}{3}$
- **b** $\frac{10}{16} = \frac{5}{\blacksquare}$
- **c** ✓ $\frac{7}{14} = \frac{1}{\blacksquare}$
- **d** $\frac{5}{8} = \frac{\blacksquare}{24}$

12 Cancel these fractions to their lowest terms.
- **a** $\frac{9}{12}$
- **b** $\frac{8}{10}$
- **c** ✓ $\frac{5}{20}$
- **d** $\frac{18}{30}$
- **e** $\frac{7}{21}$

13 Which of these fractions are in their lowest terms? $\frac{3}{6}, \frac{5}{9}, \frac{2}{10}, \frac{3}{4}, \frac{7}{9}$

14 This diagram may help you to answer the following questions.

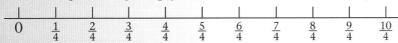

- **a** Simplify all the fractions you can on this number line. (There are five.)
- **b** Which improper fraction is equivalent to $1\frac{3}{4}$?
- **c** Which improper fraction is equivalent to $2\frac{1}{4}$?
- **d** How many quarters are equivalent to one and a half?

15 Draw a line 15 cm long and mark every centimetre in fifths. Use it to answer these questions.
- **a** How many fifths are in two whole ones?
- **b** How many fifths are in $1\frac{3}{5}$?
- **c** Change $2\frac{4}{5}$ into an improper fraction.
- **d** Change $\frac{9}{5}$ to a mixed number.

16 How many tenths are there in:
- **a** ✓ $2\frac{3}{10}$
- **b** $5\frac{1}{10}$
- **c** $8\frac{7}{10}$?

17 Change these mixed numbers to improper fractions.
- **a** $2\frac{1}{2}$
- **b** $5\frac{1}{4}$
- **c** ✓ $2\frac{3}{4}$
- **d** $4\frac{2}{5}$
- **e** $5\frac{2}{3}$

18 Write seven halves as a mixed number.

19 Show how to change $3\frac{2}{5}$ into an improper fraction.

20 Change these improper fractions to mixed numbers:

   a $\frac{10}{3}$ **b** ✓ $\frac{11}{2}$ **c** $\frac{13}{4}$ **d** $\frac{23}{10}$

   e $\frac{18}{5}$ **f** $\frac{19}{8}$ **g** $\frac{28}{9}$ **h** $\frac{23}{6}$

21 Jane had saved £18. She spent one third of her savings on a book. What was the price of the book?

22 Tom had 28 sweets. He gave one quarter of them to his friend. How many did he have left?

Consolidation Exercises

23 In this diagram $\frac{3}{4}$ of the rectangle is shaded.

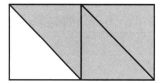

Find some more ways of showing $\frac{3}{4}$ of a rectangle.

24 Which is the odd one out in each of these sets?

   a 5 as a fraction of 10, $\frac{1}{5}$ of 10, $\frac{1}{10}$ of 5, $\frac{5}{10}$, 5 ÷ 10, 0.5

   b $\frac{1}{3}$ of 12, 12 ÷ 3, $\frac{1}{12}$ of 3, $\frac{1}{2}$ of 8, 8 ÷ 2

25 What fraction is the smaller quantity of the larger?

   a £4, £20   **b** ✓ 20 minutes, 1 hour   **c** 1 pint, 1 gallon

   d 40 mm, 8 cm   **e** 5000 g, 2 kg   **f** ✓ 70p, £7

   g 4″, 2 feet

26 How many twentieths are there in $\frac{3}{5}$?

27 Simplify the following fractions by cancelling.

   a $\frac{40}{50}$ **b** ✓ $\frac{24}{60}$ **c** $\frac{16}{40}$ **d** $\frac{50}{75}$ **e** $\frac{80}{100}$ **f** $\frac{15}{20}$ **g** $\frac{16}{48}$ **h** $\frac{32}{40}$

28 Copy these pairs of fractions and put >, <, or = between them.

a $\frac{3}{4}$ $\frac{8}{12}$ b $\frac{2}{3}$ $\frac{11}{15}$ c $\frac{5}{7}$ $\frac{15}{21}$

29 Change these improper fractions to mixed numbers.

a ✓ $\frac{22}{3}$ b $\frac{22}{7}$ c $\frac{22}{9}$ d $\frac{97}{10}$ e $\frac{39}{20}$ f $\frac{45}{15}$

30 Change these mixed numbers to improper fractions.

a ✓ $6\frac{3}{4}$ b $4\frac{3}{5}$ c $7\frac{2}{3}$ d $5\frac{3}{8}$ e $10\frac{4}{5}$ f $12\frac{3}{4}$

Challenging Exercises

31 Find some interesting ways of showing $\frac{5}{8}$ of a square.

32 Which is the odd one out in value in this set?

$\frac{1}{3} \times 2$, $\frac{2}{3}$, 10 m as a fraction of 15 m, $\frac{1}{2} \times 3$, $\frac{1}{3}$ of 2

33 Calculate:

a $\frac{1}{8}$ of £32 + $\frac{1}{2}$ of 84p   b $\frac{1}{6}$ of (27 + 15)

34 a Change $\frac{3}{4}$ and $\frac{1}{15}$ into sixtieths.

b How many times can $\frac{1}{15}$ be subtracted from $\frac{3}{4}$?

35 Find the odd one out in each of these sets.

a $\frac{12}{32}$, $\frac{4}{9}$, $\frac{3}{8}$, $\frac{15}{40}$ b $\frac{40}{60}$, $\frac{2}{3}$, $\frac{14}{21}$, $\frac{2}{7}$

36 Find two fractions, each with numerator and denominator greater than 20, equivalent to $\frac{7}{8}$.

37 Simplify these improper fractions and change them to mixed numbers.

a $\frac{44}{6}$ b $\frac{45}{12}$ c $\frac{30}{12}$ d $\frac{100}{30}$

38 Simplify these mixed numbers.

a $1\frac{9}{12}$ b $4\frac{14}{21}$ c $6\frac{30}{50}$ d $8\frac{42}{48}$

39 a Change $10\frac{2}{3}$ and $2\frac{2}{3}$ to improper fractions.

b How many times can you subtract $2\frac{2}{3}$ from $10\frac{2}{3}$? Explain your answer.

7 FRACTIONS AND DECIMALS

Essential Exercises

1 Change the following decimals to fractions.

  a 0.3   **b** 0.7   **c** ✓ 0.2   **d** 1.5

2 Find two equivalent fractions equal to 0.4.

3 **a** How many hundredths are there in 0.17?
   b Change 0.17 to a fraction.
   c Change 0.29 to a fraction.

4 Write the following decimals as fractions.

  a 0.07   **b** 0.11   **c** 0.77   **d** 2.43   **e** 3.7

5 Show how to change these decimals to fractions in their lowest terms.

  a 0.25   **b** 0.44

6 Change the following decimals to fractions in their simplest form.

  a 0.28   **b** 0.52   **c** ✓ 0.45   **d** 0.65
  e 0.04   **f** 0.15   **g** 0.55   **h** 0.36

7 Write $\frac{6}{20}$ **a** in tenths   **b** as a decimal.

8 Write $\frac{4}{5}$ **a** in tenths   **b** as a decimal.

9 Change the following fractions to decimals.

  a ✓ $\frac{2}{5}$ **b** $\frac{3}{4}$ **c** $\frac{30}{50}$ **d** $\frac{11}{50}$

10 Write these as mixed numbers in their simplest form.

  a 1.5   **b** ✓ 6.2   **c** 3.75   **d** 4.9

11 **a** Write $\frac{1}{4}$ as a decimal.   **b** Write $\frac{3}{4}$ as a decimal.   **c** Write $2\frac{3}{4}$ as a decimal.

12 You may use a diagram to answer these questions.
   a Which is bigger $\frac{1}{3}$ or $\frac{1}{4}$?   **b** Which is smaller $\frac{7}{8}$ or $\frac{5}{6}$?
   c Which is smaller $\frac{5}{12}$ or $\frac{1}{2}$?   **d** Which is bigger $\frac{5}{8}$ or $\frac{2}{3}$?
   e Write this list in order starting with the smallest: $\frac{7}{12}$, $\frac{3}{8}$, $\frac{5}{6}$.
   f Write this list in order starting with the largest: $\frac{1}{4}$, $\frac{2}{3}$, $\frac{5}{12}$.

1
+
8
10,000
÷
2/3
×
+
8
43
÷
1
10,000
×
1
4
9
16

13 Find three equal pairs in this list.

$1\frac{2}{5}$, $1\frac{1}{2}$, 1.75, 1.4, 1.3, $1\frac{3}{4}$, 1.5

Which number is the odd one out?

14 a ✓ Write this list in order starting with the smallest.

$2\frac{1}{2}$, 2.6, 2.1, $2\frac{3}{10}$

b Write this list in order starting with the largest.

3.3, $3\frac{1}{4}$, 3.7, $3\frac{1}{2}$

15 Copy each pair and put > or < between them.
a $\frac{1}{2}$ 0.6   **b** ✓ 0.25 $\frac{1}{3}$ **c** $\frac{3}{4}$ 0.9

16 Copy each pair and put > or < between them.
a $\frac{1}{2}$ $\frac{1}{3}$ **b** ✓ $\frac{3}{4}$ $\frac{7}{10}$ **c** $\frac{5}{8}$ $\frac{4}{5}$

17 Which package is heavier, a square one weighing 2.8 kg or a round one weighing $2\frac{3}{4}$ kg?

18 A beech tree is $16\frac{1}{2}$ m tall and an oak is 16.45 m tall. Which tree is taller?

Consolidation Exercises

19 Change the following decimal numbers to mixed numbers.
a ✓ 2.1   **b** 5.3   **c** 1.35   **d** 3.12

20 Change the following decimal numbers to mixed numbers in their simplest form.
a ✓ 4.8   **b** 9.6   **c** 10.35   **d** 2.65

21 Change the following mixed numbers to decimal numbers.
a ✓ $7\frac{1}{10}$ **b** $3\frac{1}{5}$ **c** $5\frac{1}{4}$ **d** $4\frac{3}{5}$

22 Which is smaller $2\frac{1}{3}$ or $2\frac{1}{4}$?

23 Copy these and put > or < between them.

  a $\frac{1}{4}$ 0.26   **b** ✓ 0.51 $\frac{1}{2}$ **c** $\frac{3}{10}$ 0.29   **d** $2\frac{3}{4}$ 2.8   **e** $3\frac{1}{2}$ 3.52

24 Write each of these sets of numbers in order starting with the smallest:

  a $\frac{17}{4}$, $4\frac{1}{2}$, $\frac{49}{10}$ **b** $4\frac{1}{3}$, 4.3, $4\frac{1}{2}$, 4.25

25 Sue walks $1\frac{2}{5}$ km to school and John cycles 1.3 km. Whose journey is shorter? Explain your answer.

Challenging Exercises

26 True or false?

  a $2\frac{3}{5} = 2.3$ **b** $8\frac{1}{2} = 8.5$ **c** $5\frac{1}{4} = 5.4$

  d $\frac{27}{10} = 2.7$ **e** $\frac{7}{100} = 0.7$ **f** 1 hour 15 minutes = 1.15 hours

  If you think they are false explain why.

27 Change the following to mixed numbers.

  a 3.12   **b** 4.88   **c** 10.56

  d 7.42   **e** 9.125   **f** 2.375

28 Use equivalent fractions to find which is bigger in each of these pairs.

  a $\frac{2}{3}$ or $\frac{5}{6}$ **b** $\frac{3}{10}$ or $\frac{2}{5}$ **c** $\frac{7}{12}$ or $\frac{3}{4}$

29 Change the following fractions to twentieths and put them in order starting with the smallest.

  $\frac{3}{4}$, $\frac{9}{10}$, $\frac{4}{5}$, $\frac{38}{40}$

30 Change the fractions in these lists to decimals and then write each set of numbers in order, starting with the smallest.

  a $\frac{3}{4}$, $\frac{4}{5}$, 0.7, 0.85   **b** $1\frac{3}{5}$, $1\frac{1}{2}$, 1.55, $1\frac{13}{20}$

31 Copy these and put > or < or = between them.

  a $\frac{15}{20}$ 0.74   **b** $\frac{4}{5}$ 0.8   **c** $2\frac{1}{5}$ 2.22   **d** $3\frac{1}{10}$ 3.09

1
+
8
10,000
÷
2/3
×
+
8
43
÷
1
10,000
×
1
4
9
16

ADDING AND SUBTRACTING FRACTIONS

Essential Exercises

1 State whether the following is true or false.

$$\frac{1}{4} + \frac{1}{4} = \frac{2}{8}$$

Draw a diagram to explain your answer.

2 Work out:

a $\frac{1}{5} + \frac{2}{5}$ b $\frac{2}{9} + \frac{5}{9}$ c $\frac{1}{11} + \frac{3}{11} + \frac{4}{11}$

3 Copy and complete this table for adding fractions.

+	$\frac{1}{7}$	$\frac{4}{7}$
$\frac{3}{7}$		
$\frac{2}{7}$		

4 Work out the following and simplify your answers.

a $\frac{1}{8} + \frac{3}{8}$ b $\frac{3}{10} + \frac{5}{10}$ c ✓ $\frac{1}{9} + \frac{5}{9}$

d $\frac{5}{12} + \frac{7}{12}$ e $\frac{1}{6} + \frac{2}{6} + \frac{3}{6}$ f $\frac{1}{8} + \frac{2}{8} + \frac{3}{8}$

5 Work out the following and change your answers to a mixed number.

a $\frac{3}{7} + \frac{5}{7} + \frac{1}{7}$ b ✓ $\frac{3}{8} + \frac{3}{8} + \frac{5}{8}$ c $\frac{1}{10} + \frac{3}{10} + \frac{7}{10}$ d $\frac{5}{12} + \frac{11}{12} + \frac{1}{12}$

6 Work out and simplify:

a $\frac{5}{8} - \frac{3}{8}$ b $\frac{7}{10} - \frac{2}{10}$ c $\frac{5}{6} - \frac{1}{6}$ d ✓ $\frac{7}{9} - \frac{4}{9}$

7 Work out the following and change your answers to mixed numbers, simplified where possible.

a $\frac{4}{9} + \frac{7}{9}$ b $\frac{2}{5} + \frac{3}{5} + \frac{4}{5}$ c $\frac{3}{8} + \frac{7}{8}$ d $\frac{3}{5} + \frac{3}{5} + \frac{3}{5}$

8 Work out the following and simplify your answers, where possible, by cancelling.

a $\frac{2}{11} + \frac{7}{11}$ b $\frac{2}{9} + \frac{4}{9}$ c $\frac{1}{10} + \frac{2}{10} + \frac{3}{10}$

d $\frac{4}{5} - \frac{2}{5}$ e $\frac{5}{7} - \frac{1}{7}$ f $\frac{5}{8} - \frac{3}{8}$

9 a Calculate $\frac{8}{11} - \frac{2}{11} - \frac{2}{11} - \frac{2}{11} - \frac{2}{11}$.

b How many times can $\frac{2}{11}$ be subtracted from $\frac{8}{11}$?

Consolidation Exercises

10 🏠 Work out the following and give your answers in their simplest form.

   a $\frac{1}{8} + \frac{5}{8}$ **b** $\frac{1}{12} + \frac{5}{12}$ **c** ✓ $\frac{2}{9} + \frac{3}{9} + \frac{4}{9}$ **d** $\frac{1}{8} + \frac{5}{8} + \frac{7}{8}$ **e** $\frac{3}{6} + \frac{4}{6} + \frac{5}{6}$

11 Work out the following and give your answers in their simplest form.

   a $\frac{11}{14} - \frac{5}{14}$ **b** $\frac{5}{6} - \frac{1}{6}$ **c** $\frac{9}{10} - \frac{3}{10}$ **d** $\frac{11}{12} - \frac{7}{12}$ **e** ✓ $1 - \frac{3}{8}$

12 a Change $\frac{1}{4}$ into eighths.   **b** Calculate $\frac{1}{4} + \frac{3}{8}$.

13 a Change $\frac{1}{5}$ into tenths.   **b** Calculate $\frac{1}{5} + \frac{7}{10}$.

14 a Calculate $\frac{2}{7} + \frac{2}{7} + \frac{2}{7}$.   **b** Copy and complete $\frac{2}{7} \times \blacksquare = \frac{6}{7}$.

15 Work out $\frac{2}{9} \times 4$.

Challenging Exercises

16 Work out the following and give your answers in their simplest form.

   a $\frac{4}{5} + \frac{2}{5} - \frac{3}{5}$ **b** $\frac{7}{8} - \frac{5}{8} + \frac{1}{8}$ **c** $\frac{5}{9} + \frac{7}{9} - \frac{2}{9}$

   d $\frac{5}{6} + \frac{3}{6} - \frac{4}{6}$ **e** $\frac{11}{12} - \frac{5}{12} + \frac{7}{12}$ **f** $\frac{11}{15} + \frac{13}{15} - \frac{4}{15}$

17 a Calculate $\frac{2}{3} + \frac{2}{3} + \frac{2}{3} + \frac{2}{3}$.   **b** What is $\frac{2}{3} \times 4$?

18 a Change $\frac{3}{5}$ into tenths.   **b** Calculate $\frac{3}{5} + \frac{3}{10}$.

19 a Change $\frac{3}{4}$ and $\frac{2}{3}$ into twelfths.   **b** Calculate $\frac{3}{4} - \frac{2}{3}$.

20 How many times can $\frac{1}{2}$ be subtracted from $2\frac{1}{2}$?

21 🏠 Work out $5\frac{1}{2} \div \frac{1}{2}$.

22 🖾 Jeremy drinks $\frac{1}{5}$ of a carton of fruit juice each day. How long will a pack of 4 cartons last?

FRACTIONS AND INTEGERS

1 What is $\frac{1}{4}$ of 24?

2 Find: **a** $\frac{1}{3}$ of 15 and $\frac{2}{3}$ of 15 **b** $\frac{1}{4}$ of 20 and $\frac{3}{4}$ of 20
c $\frac{1}{4}$ of 28 and $\frac{3}{4}$ of 28 **d** $\frac{1}{10}$ of 60 and $\frac{7}{10}$ of 60

3 Find: **a** $\frac{2}{3}$ of 24 **b** $\frac{3}{8}$ of 16 **c** ✓ $\frac{4}{5}$ of 15

4 Calculate: **a** $\frac{1}{5}$ of £20 and $\frac{3}{5}$ of £20 **b** $\frac{1}{8}$ of 40 kg and $\frac{3}{8}$ of 40 kg

5 Which is the odd one out in each of these sets? Explain why.
a $\frac{1}{2}$ of 14, 14 ÷ 2, $\frac{1}{2} \times 14$, 2 × 14 **b** $\frac{1}{4}$ of 20, 20 ÷ 4, 20 × 4, $\frac{1}{4} \times 20$

6 a Find $\frac{1}{5} + \frac{1}{5} + \frac{1}{5}$. **b** What is $\frac{1}{5} \times 3$?

7 Calculate: **a** a) $\frac{1}{7} \times 6$ **b** $3 \times \frac{1}{8}$ **c** ✓ $5 \times \frac{2}{3}$

8 Change these decimals to fractions and work out:
a 0.5 × 14 **b** 0.2 × 20 **c** 0.3 × 50.

9 Find two pairs equal in value. Which is the odd one out?

12 ÷ 3, 3 as a fraction of 12, $\frac{1}{4}$ of 12, $\frac{1}{3} \times 12$, $3 \times \frac{1}{12}$

10 Find:
a $\frac{3}{5}$ of 35 m **b** $\frac{7}{8}$ of 80 cm **c** ✓ $\frac{3}{4}$ of £36
d $\frac{5}{6}$ of 30 g **e** $\frac{3}{8}$ of 56 **f** $\frac{2}{3}$ of 24

11 Work out:
a $\frac{1}{10}$ of 1 km **b** $\frac{9}{10}$ of 1 km **c** ✓ $\frac{7}{10}$ of 1 kg
d $\frac{3}{10}$ of 1 metre? **e** $\frac{3}{10}$ of 2 m **f** $\frac{7}{100}$ of 1 kg.

12 A bag contained 36 sweets. One-third were red and one-quarter were green. The rest were yellow. How many yellow sweets were there in the bag?

13 A box contained 32 chocolates. Three-eighths had soft centres. How many had soft centres?

14 A man earned £16 an hour. How much would he earn in $\frac{3}{4}$ hour?

Consolidation Exercises

15 🏠 Which is the odd one out in each of these sets? Explain why.

a ✓ $\frac{1}{5}$ of 15, 15 ÷ 5, 0.2 × 15, $\frac{1}{5}$ × 15, $\frac{15}{2}$

b $\frac{1}{2}$ of 24, $\frac{1}{2}$ × 24, 0.5 of 24, 24 ÷ 2, $\frac{2}{24}$

c $\frac{1}{8}$ of 40, $\frac{8}{40}$, $\frac{1}{8}$ × 40, $\frac{40}{8}$, 40 ÷ 8

d $\frac{3}{5}$ of 20, $\frac{20}{3}$ × 5, 3 × 20 ÷ 5, 3 × 0.2 × 20

e $\frac{2}{3}$ of 12, $\frac{2}{3}$ × 12, $\frac{12}{2}$ × 3, 2 × 12 ÷ 3, $\frac{12}{3}$ × 2

16 Find two pairs equal in value. Which is the odd one out?

$\frac{3}{5}$ of 10, $\frac{5}{3}$, $\frac{3}{10}$ of 5, $\frac{3}{5}$ × 10, 0.3 × 5

17 🧩 In a class of 30 children $\frac{3}{5}$ had blue eyes. How many children had blue eyes?

18 🧩 The summer holidays last for 45 days. If it rains on $\frac{2}{9}$ of the days how many wet days are there?

Challenging Exercises

19 Find three pairs equal in value. Which is the odd one out?

$\frac{4}{5}$ × 10, 4 × $\frac{5}{10}$, 0.4 × 10, $\frac{4}{10}$ of 5, 0.8 × 5, 10 ÷ 4 × 5, 4 × 10 ÷ 5

20 Which is bigger:

    a $\frac{5}{8}$ of 56 or $\frac{3}{4}$ of 52   b 0.4 × 30 or $\frac{1}{3}$ of 33

    c 2.4 × 20 or $\frac{1}{4}$ of 200   d $\frac{2}{3}$ of 24 or $\frac{3}{4}$ × 11?

21 🏠 Copy these pairs and put > or < or = between them.

    a $\frac{7}{8}$ × 72   0.9 × 80   b 280 ÷ 20 × 3 $\frac{3}{5}$ of 75

    c $\frac{7}{10}$ of 4 m   4.8 × 50 cm   d 0.3 × £2 $\frac{7}{8}$ of 72p

PERCENTAGE, FRACTION, DECIMAL EQUIVALENTS

Essential Exercises

1 Copy and complete the following:

   a $30\% = \frac{\blacksquare}{100} = \frac{\blacksquare}{10}$ **b** $25\% = \frac{25}{\blacksquare} = \frac{1}{\blacksquare}$ **c** $40\% = \frac{40}{\blacksquare} = \frac{\blacksquare}{5}$ **d** $\blacksquare\% = \frac{7}{100}$

2 Write these percentages as fractions in their lowest terms.

   a 70%   **b** 75%   **c** ✓ 80%   **d** 3%   **e** 85%   **f** $66\frac{2}{3}\%$

3 **a** Write 160% as an improper fraction in its lowest terms.

   b Write your answer to **a** as a mixed number.

   c Write 150% as a mixed number.

4 Change these percentages to mixed numbers.

   a 175%   **b** ✓ 120%   **c** 109%

5 Copy and complete the following:

   a $\frac{1}{5} = \frac{\blacksquare}{100} = \blacksquare\%$ **b** $\frac{3}{4} = \frac{\blacksquare}{100} = \blacksquare\%$ **c** $2\frac{1}{2} = \frac{\blacksquare}{2} = \frac{\blacksquare}{200} = \frac{\blacksquare}{100} = \blacksquare\%$

   d $0.7 = \frac{7}{\blacksquare} = \frac{\blacksquare}{100} = \blacksquare\%$ **e** $0.03 = \frac{3}{\blacksquare} = \blacksquare\%$

6 Change these decimals first to fractions with denominator 100, and then to percentages.

   a 0.63   **b** 0.1   **c** ✓ 0.3   **d** 1.74

7 Change these percentages to decimals:

   a 37%   **b** ✓ 40%   **c** 8%   **d** 173%

8 Which is the biggest in this list: 0.43, 50%, $\frac{1}{3}$?

9 Copy and complete the following table:

Fraction	Percentage	Decimal
$\frac{1}{5}$		
	75%	
		0.7
	60%	
$\frac{9}{20}$		
		0.05

Consolidation Exercises

10 Change these percentages to fractions in their simplest form.

    a 40%   **b** 15%   **c** 103%   **d** 180%

11 Change these percentages to decimals.

    a 60%   **b** 130%   **c** 274%

12 🏠 Change these decimals to percentages.

    a 0.73   **b** 0.07   **c** $\frac{1}{2}$ **d** $\frac{2}{5}$ **e** $\frac{3}{10}$

13 Write these fractions as equivalent fractions with denominator 100 and then as percentages.

    a $\frac{23}{50}$ **b** $\frac{2}{5}$ **c** ✓ $\frac{7}{20}$ **d** $3\frac{1}{2}$

14 Change these fractions to percentages.

    a $\frac{9}{20}$ **b** ✓ $\frac{17}{20}$ **c** $1\frac{19}{100}$

    d $\frac{31}{50}$ **e** $\frac{4}{25}$ **f** $3\frac{1}{5}$

15 Copy and complete the following.

    a $\frac{2}{8} = \frac{1}{4} = \blacksquare\%$ and so $\frac{1}{8} = \blacksquare\%$ **b** $\frac{68}{200} = \frac{\blacksquare}{100} = \blacksquare\%$

16 Which is the smallest in this list: $\frac{3}{10}$, 0.4, or 25% ?

Challenging Exercises

17 Write each of these as a mixed number or whole number.

    a 2.03   **b** 4.72   **c** 11.33   **d** 500%

18 **a** Change $2\frac{1}{3}$ to a decimal.   **b** Change $2\frac{1}{3}$ to a percentage.

19 **a** Write down $\frac{3}{4}$ as a percentage.

    b What is the percentage equivalent of $\frac{3}{8}$?

20 🏠 Find the biggest in each of these lists.

    a 0.47, 53%, $\frac{3}{5}$ **b** 4.1, 401%, $4\frac{1}{8}$ **c** 109%, $1\frac{1}{10}$, 0.9

FINDING A PERCENTAGE OF ...

Essential Exercises

1 Find 10% of each of these.
   a 120   **b** ✓ £900   **c** 70 kg   **d** 2000 m   **e** £86

2 Use your answers to question **1** to find 5% of these.
   a 120   **b** £900   **c** 70 kg   **d** 2000 m   **e** £86

3 Find 5% of these.
   a 60   **b** £180   **c** 400 km   **d** 260 cm   **e** 640 g

4 ✓ Find: **a** 10% of 80 cm.   **b** 5% of 80 cm.
   c Use your answers to **a** and **b** to find 15% of 80 cm.

5 Find 15% of these.
   a £20   **b** 800   **c** 320 g   **d** £30   **e** 26 m

6 What is 100% of these?
   a 9 kg   **b** 25 km   **c** £87   **d** £100   **e** £4000

7 Find: **a** 10% of 800 m   **b** 1% of 800 m.
   c Use your answers to **a** and **b** to find 11% of 800 m.

8 ✓ Find: **a** 10% of 40 m   **b** 30% of 40 m   **c** 80% of 40 m.

9 Work out: **a** 30% of £60   **b** 40% of 90 cm   **c** 70% of 50p.

10 a What is 50% of 80?   **b** Write down 10% of 80.
   c Use your answers to **a** and **b** to find 60% of 80.

11 A girl weighs 44 kg. Her brother is 25% heavier.
   a How much heavier is her brother?
   b What does her brother weigh?

12 In a sale prices are reduced by 10%. Rachel bought some shoes which had cost £40 before the sale.
   a How much was the reduction?
   b What did Rachel pay for the shoes?

13 Find 5% of these. **a** 240 **b** £248

14 Find:
   a 10% of £220 **b** 5% of £220 **c** 15% of £220

15 Calculate 15% of £80.

16 🏠 Calculate these:
   a 10% of 70 **b** 30% of 70 **c** 60% of £120 **d** 30% of £130

17 Work out 11% of £2300.

Consolidation Exercises

18 Find 15% of these.
   a 620 **b** £2800 **c** 486 kg **d** 360° **e** 130 g

19 ✓ **a** Write down 100% of £700.
   b Find 1% of £700.
   c Work out 99% of £700.

Challenging Exercises

20 Calculate:
   a 30% of 310 **b** 40% of £1250 **c** 60% of 21 kg.

21 Find: **a** 100% of 340 m **b** 10% of 340 m **c** 90% of 340 m.

22 Work out 11% of 250.

23 Calculate:
   a 1% of 1200 **b** 99% of 1200 g **c** 25% of 1200 m **d** 26% of £1200.

24 🔲 🏠 A school has 1650 pupils. On Friday 2% were absent. How many pupils were absent?

PERCENTAGES WITH A CALCULATOR

Essential Exercises

1 In each of the following first write the percentages as decimals then use a calculator to work out the answer.

  a 16% of 55   **b** ✓ 28% of 12

  c 98% of 36   **d** 56% of 123 cm

2 **a** Write down a fraction calculation for working out 16% of 275.

  b Write down, in order, the calculator keys needed for your calculation.

  c Use your answer to **b** and a calculator to find 16% of 275.

3 Use an efficient calculator method to work out the following percentages.

  a 48% of £26   **b** ✓ 23% of £64

  c 53% of £28   **d** 87% of £44

  e 22% of 65   **f** 46% of £75

  g 89% of 98 m   **h** 37% of £320

4 **a** Describe how to find a sensible estimate for working out 51% of any amount.

  b What is 39 to the nearest 10?

  c Write down a calculation for estimating 51% of 39 and work out the estimate.

  d Use a calculator to work out 51% of 39.

5 **a** Write down a decimal calculation for working out 62% of 38.

  b Use a calculator to work out your calculation.

6 In each of the following first write the percentages as decimals then use a calculator to work out the answer.

  a 46% of 24 m   **b** 71% of 42 kg

Consolidation Exercises

7 **a** Describe a mental method for finding a sensible estimate for working out 49% of any amount.

b What is 58 to the nearest 10?

c Write down a calculation for estimating 49% of 58 and work out the estimate.

d Use a calculator to work out 49% of 58.

8 **a** Estimate the value of 51% of £81.

b Use a calculator to find the value of 51% of £81.

9 Find as many different ways as you can to work out 16% of 75.
At least one method should not use a calculator.
Which of your ways is the most efficient?

10 Use a calculator to work out the difference between 47% of 93 and 93% of 47. Explain your answer.

11 **a** Write down three different calculator methods for working out 78% of 63.

b Which is the least efficient method?

c What is 78% of 63?

Challenging Exercises

12 **a** Write down 112% as a decimal.

b Write down a decimal calculation for working out 112% of 38.

c Use a calculator to work out your calculation.

13 **a** Describe a mental method for finding an estimate for working out 24% of any amount.

b What is 158 to the nearest 10?

c Write down a calculation for estimating 24% of 58 and work out the estimate.

d Use a calculator to work out 24% of 58.

14 First estimate and then use a calculator to work out:

    a 24% of 122   **b** 26% of 79   **c** 19% of 37

    d 51% of 386   **e** 49% of £450   **f** 24% of £794

1 + 8 10,000 ÷ 2/3 × + 8 43 ÷ 1 10,000 × 1 4 9 16

RATIO AND PROPORTION 7

1 Buttons are sold on cards with five buttons on each.
If I need 15 buttons how many cards should I buy?

2 One roll of freezer bags has 50 bags on it.
  a How many similar rolls should I buy if I need 150 bags.
  b How many bags are there on 6 rolls?

3 ✓ A packet of cereals contains twelve servings.
  a How many servings are in three similar packets?
  b How many packets are needed for 48 servings?

4 Five boxes of chocolates cost £20.
  a What is the cost of one box?   **b** What is the cost of three boxes?

5 In a box of 40 chocolates 24 have hard centres and 16 have soft centres.
  a What fraction of the chocolates have hard centres?
  b What proportion of the chocolates have hard centres?
  c What percentage of the chocolates have hard centres?

6 In a class there are 12 boys and 18 girls. Write these ratios in their simplest form.
  a number of boys : number of girls
  b number of girls : number of boys
  c number of boys : total number of children
  d What fraction of the children are boys?

7 Simplify these ratios.
  a $5:15$ **b** $6:8$ **c** ✓ $20:30$ **d** $25:50$

8 £40 is shared between Neil and Beth in ratio $1:3$.
  a What fraction does Neil get?   **b** ✓ How much money does he get?
  c What fraction does Beth get?   **d** How much money does she get?

9 The ratio of round biscuits to square biscuits in a box of mixed biscuits
is $2:3$. There are 50 biscuits in the box.
  a How many are round?   **b** How many are square?

10 🏠 At a birthday party there are 4 children to each adult.
There are five adults at the party.
  a How many children are there?
  b How many people are there altogether?
  c What fraction of people are adults?
  d Write down the ratio of children to adults.
  e What percentage of the people at the party are adults?
  f What percentage are children?

Consolidation Exercises

11 🔲 A plan of a room is drawn using a scale of 1 cm to 50 cm. The room is 8 m long. What distance is this on the plan?

12 🔲 ✓ A recipe for soup for 4 people uses 16 ounces of onions. What weight of onions would be needed to make the soup for 10 people?

13 🔲 Orange paint is made by mixing red and yellow paint in the ratio 1 : 3. A tin contains 800 ml of orange paint. How much of each colour paint is there?

14 🔲 ✓ On my holiday the ratio of wet days to dry days was 1 : 4. My holiday lasted 10 days. How many wet days were there?

15 🔲 In a group of 20 girls 12 played netball on Monday and the rest played hockey. What was the ratio of netball players to hockey players?

Challenging Exercises

16 Simplify these ratios. **a** 140 : 210   **b** 2800 : 2000   **c** 1.5 : 3.5

17 🔲 Lyn is 6 years old and Tim is 10 years old. Divide £40 between Lyn and Tim in the ratio of their ages.

18 🔲 🏠 In a recipe for shortbread biscuits the ratio of fat to flour to sugar is 2 : 3 : 1. If they contain 3 ounces of sugar how much fat and flour do they contain?

POWERS OF TEN

Essential Exercises

1 What is the value of 10^3?

2 Write one million as a power of 10.

3 Write $10 \times 10 \times 10 \times 10 \times 10$ as a power of 10 and work out the value.

4 Write 4×10^4 in words and work out the value.

5 Write down the value of:
  a 6×10^5 **b** ✓ 0.004×10^3 **c** 2.3×10^2

6 Add 0.001 to each of the following.
  a 1.019   **b** 3.509   **c** 3.999

7 Write down the value of A in each of these.
  a $3.482 + A = 3.489$ **b** $5.629 - A = 5.624$
  c $9.604 - A = 9.004$ **d** ✓ $5.437 - A = 5.407$

8 a Work out 7×0.01.   **b** Write $7 \div 100$ as a decimal number.
  c What do you notice about your answers?   **d** Explain why this happens.

9 How many tenths are there in these?
  a 4   **b** ✓ 4.1   **c** 40   **d** 0.4

10 How many hundredths are there in these?
  a 0.02   **b** 2   **c** 0.2   **d** 20   **e** 0.22

11 a Work out $6 \div 0.1$.   **b** Write down the value of 6×10.
  c What do you notice about your answers?   **d** Explain why this happens.

12 Find two equal pairs from this list. $2 \div 0.1$ 2×100 $2 \div 0.01$ 2×10

13 Write these as a multiplication and then write down the answers.
  a $5 \div 0.1$ **b** $8 \div 0.01$

14 Find two equal pairs from this list.
  $0.3 \times 100,\ 30,\ 0.03 \times 10,\ 3,\ 0.3.$

  Which is the odd one out?

15 The bank interest rate falls by 0.01% from 4.30%. What is the new rate?

Consolidation Exercises

16 Write down the value of these.

    a 4×10^2 **b** 7×10^6 **c** 8×10^5 **d** 2×10^1

17 Write 2.6×10^2 in words and work out the value.

18 Write down the value of these.

    a 4.75×10^2 **b** 2.7×10^2 **c** ✓ 5.365×10^3 **d** 6.98×10^3

19 🏠 Calculate these:

    a $7.269 + 0.001$ **b** ✓ $8.989 + 0.002$ **c** $4 - 0.006$

    d $3 - 0.003$ **e** $4 - 0.009$ **f** $0.2 - 0.001$

20 For each of the following pairs find the difference.

    a 2.745 2.795   **b** 6.941 6.947   **c** 7.236 7.242

21 Calculate:

    a 0.4×0.2 **b** ✓ 0.7×0.1 **c** 0.5×0.2

    d $0.8 \div 0.01$ **e** $0.5 \div 0.001$ **f** $0.6 \div 0.01$

Challenging Exercises

22 Work out the value of A in each of these.

    a $3.992 + A = 4.692$ **b** $7.039 + A = 7.119$

    c $5.951 - A = 5.943$ **d** $2.034 - A = 1.984$

23 What must be added to the first number to make the second in these pairs?

    a 3.478 to 3.487   **b** 6.349 to 6.357

    c 4.592 to 4.602   **d** 7.998 to 8.002

24 Calculate:

    a $4 - 0.001$ **b** $6.4 - 0.01$ **c** $5.3 - 0.001$ **d** $5.1 - 0.005$

    e 5×0.002 **f** 0.001×20 **g** 4×0.03 **h** 0.6×0.01

    i $0.8 \div 0.02$ **j** $9 \div 0.03$ **k** $4 \div 0.001$ **l** $6 \div 0.003$

    m $(4.77 + 0.06) \times 100$ **n** $5.274 \times 10 + 0.08$ **o** $7 \div (2.583 - 2.582)$

25 🔲 🏠 Write down a calculation with brackets for which the answer is 1.23. (Try to find more than one way.)

Side bar: 1 + 8 10,000 ÷ 2/3 × + 8 43 ÷ 1 10,000 × 1 4 9 16

ORDERING DECIMALS

1 Write down the numbers indicated by the arrows on this number line.

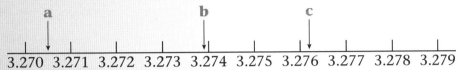

a   b   c

3.270   3.271   3.272   3.273   3.274   3.275   3.276   3.277   3.278   3.279

2 Write down the next three terms in these sequences.

   a   0.245, 0.250, 0.255, …, …, …   **b**   3.252, 3.254, 3.256, …, …, …

3 Copy these pairs and put > or < or = between them.

   a   0.702   0.77   **b**   0.482   0.248   **c** ✓ 3.841   3.814   **d**   7.036   7.36

   e   0.764 m   67.4 cm   **f**   365 mg   0.365 g   **g**   −4.281 −4.812

4 Write these lists in order starting with the smallest.

   a   0.753, 0.573, 0.057 3, 0.350 7   **b**   5.836, 5.083, 6.736, 5.306

   c   0.42, 0.24. 0.042, 0.402   **d**   0.511 6, 0.561 1, 0.516 1, 0.651 1, 0.611 5

5 Find the number halfway between these pairs.

   a   0.06 and 0.07   **b**   8.04 and 8.05   **c**   3.002 and 3.004

   d ✓ 2.764 and 2.766   **e**   3.412 m and 3.612 m   **f**   −0.4 and −0.8

6 🔦 I could buy a roll of carpet 4.675 m long. My hall is 4.765 m long.
Is the roll of carpet too long or too short? By how much?

7 🔦 The contents of seven lemonade bottles were measured and these are the
results recorded in litres.

> 1.966,   1.947,   2.029,   1.984,   2.009,   1.999,   2.021

   a   Arrange these numbers in increasing order.

   b   The middle one in the ordered list is the median value.
       What is the median amount of lemonade correct to two decimal places?

8 🔦 The weights of seven packets of cereals were recorded in kilograms.

> 0.738,   0.732,   0.729,   0.743,   0.741,   0.730,   0.740

List these weights in order starting with the heaviest.

9 Find the smallest and largest numbers from this set and then add them together.

> 0.070 8, 0.009 78, 0.005 307, 0.080 7

10 ✓ Arrange these in decreasing order.

> 0.620 5, 0.065 2, 0.625 0, 0.652 01, 0.650 2

11 🏠 Write down the next three terms in these sequences.
  a 0.103, 0.143, 0.183, …, …, …
  b 4.428 9, 4.428 7, 4.428 5, …, …, …

12 The number 2.549 is halfway between 2.546 and a second number. What is the second number?

13 Measure the arm span a of 20 pupils. Write down the measurements in metres to the nearest centimetre. Construct a grouped frequency table for your measurements using groups such as:

> $1.30\,\text{m} \leqslant a < 1.35\,\text{m}$ $1.35\,\text{m} \leqslant a < 1.4\,\text{m}$ $1.4\,\text{m} \leqslant a < 1.45\,\text{m}$

Challenging Exercises

14 Find the difference between the smallest and largest numbers in this set.

> 1.009 009, 1.909 909, 1.090 090, 0.999 999

15 Find these values and then arrange them in increasing order.
  a $0.006\,53 \times 100$, $7002 \div 1000$, 0.056×10, $0.000\,006\,05 \times 10^6$
  b $0.207\,3 \times 10$, $0.023\,7 \times 100$, $2703 \div 10$, $0.023\,07 \times 10^3$

16 🏠 Work out these values and then arrange the four answers in ascending order of size.
  a 0.786×10^3
  b $7.142\,8 \times 10^2$
  c $1.078\,04 \times 10^3$
  d $(7.073 + 0.006) \times 100$

ROUNDING 8

Essential Exercises

Country	Area (km^2)	Population (in millions)
United Kingdom	243 300	58.97
Ireland	70 300	3.619
France	552 000	58.805
Germany	357 000	82.079
USA	9 373 000	270.29
Barbados	430	0.259
Singapore	620	3.49
Christmas Island	140	0.002
China	9 597 000	1 236.915

Use the information in this table to answer these questions.

1 What is the area of the United Kingdom correct to the nearest million km^2?

2 ✓ What is the area of Ireland correct to the nearest thousand km^2?

3 What is the area of India correct to the nearest ten thousand?

4 Which country has the largest area? What is its area correct to the nearest million?

5 What is the area of France correct to the nearest hundred thousand?

6 Which two countries have equal populations when rounded to the nearest million?

7 What is the population correct to the nearest million of:
   a Ireland **b** USA **c** UK?

8 ✓ Write down the populations of France and of Germany in millions correct to two decimal places.

9 Which country has a population less than 250 000?

10 ✓ Round 72.956 correct to:

   a two decimal places   **b** one decimal place   **c** the nearest whole number.

11 Round 4.249 correct to:

   a two decimal places   **b** one decimal place.

12 🖩 Write the fractions $\frac{1}{3}, \frac{5}{6}, \frac{2}{9}, \frac{7}{9}, \frac{4}{11}$

   a as recurring decimals   **b** correct to two decimal places.

13 In the table on page 49 the areas are given correct to the nearest thousand.

   a ✓ What is the least the area of France could be?

   b What is the most the area of Germany could be?

   c Use appropriate approximations to estimate the total area of France and Germany. Justify your answer.

14 Use appropriate approximations of the values given in the table on page 49 to estimate the total population of the United Kingdom and Ireland. Justify your answer.

15 The population of China given in the table on page 49 can be written as $1.236\,915 \times 10^n$. What is the value of n?

16 Find the total population of the European countries in the table on page 49. Give your answer correct to the nearest:

   a million   **b** hundred million.

17 🖩 🏠 Use a calculator and information in the table on page 49 to find, for Barbados, Singapore, and Christmas Island:

   a the mean value of the areas to the nearest ten thousand

   b the populations in millions correct to two decimal places.

18 **a** Work out $2 \div 7$ giving the first nine non-zero digits in your answer.

   b Write down $\frac{2}{7}$ as a decimal correct to two decimal places.

POSITIVE AND NEGATIVE INTEGERS (ADDING AND SUBTRACTING)

Essential Exercises

1 Calculate:

a $7 + -4$	**b** $9 + -8$	**c** $4 + -4$	**d** $2 + -5$	**e** $6 + -9$
f $-2 + 7$	**g** $-5 + 3$	**h** ✓ $-8 + 9$	**i** $-9 + 8$	**j** $-3 + 9$
k $-3 + -6$	**l** $-4 + -2$	**m** ✓ $-7 + -5$	**n** $-8 + -8$	**o** $-7 + -9$
p $6 - -2$	**q** $8 - -5$	**r** ✓ $4 - -7$	**s** $2 - -4$	**t** $1 - -9$
u $-1 - -3$	**v** $-5 - -2$	**w** $-4 - -8$	**x** $-3 - -3$	**y** $-7 - -5$

2 Write down the value of A in each of these.

    a $5 - A = 6$ **b** $-4 + A = 3$ **c** $7 + A = 2$ **d** $-6 + A = -4$

    e $-8 - A = -3$ **f** $-7 + A = -9$ **g** $5 + A = -5$ **h** $7 - A = 13$

3 Work out all these answers to find which is the odd one out.

    $2 + -7$ $-8 + 3$ $3 - -2$ $-9 - -4$

4 Calculate:

    a $20 + -30$ **b** $-40 + 10$ **c** ✓ $-10 - -10$ **d** $51 - -8$ **e** $29 + -4$

    f $6 + -17$ **g** $24 + -24$ **h** $-13 + -13$ **i** $-3 + -15$ **j** $-11 - -11$

5 If $x = -5$ and $y = -8$ work out the value of these.

    a $x + y$ **b** $x - y$ **c** $y - x$ **d** $x + x$ **e** $y + y$

6 Copy and complete this magic square.

-4	6	-5
3		

7 Calculate:

a $-7 + -6$ **b** $9 - -5$ **c** ✓ $-4 - -7$ **d** $-9 + -11$

e $7 + -10$ **f** $12 + -8$ **g** $-14 + -4$ **h** $7 + -13$

i $-17 + -9$ **j** ✓ $-9 + -9$ **k** $-20 + -5$ **l** $99 - -6$

m $103 + -7$ **n** $-0.6 + -0.3$ **o** $1.5 - -0.6$ **p** $-0.4 + -1$

8 Write down the value of A in each of these.

a $-17 + A = -13$ **b** $8 + A = -4$ **c** $-7 + A = -12$

d $19 + A = -2$ **e** $-11 - A = 4$

9 If $a = -2$, $b = -9$ and $c = 8$ work out these.

a $a + b$ **b** $a - b$ **c** $c + a$ **d** $b - c$ **e** $a + b + c$

10 Calculate:

a $-4 + -9 - -2$ **b** $6 - -8 + -5$ **c** $12 + -7 - -5$

d $-16 + -6 - -9$ **e** $7 - -11 + -16$ **f** $-104 + 108$

g $-11 + -11 + -11$ **h** $-99 - -102$ **i** $50 + -11 + -9$

j $-0.7 + -0.5 - -0.3$ **k** $1.4 + -1.2$ **l** $71 + -71$

m $123 + -125$ **n** $6 - (5 + -3)$ **o** $-4 - (8 + -2)$

p $(6 + -10) - (3 - -7)$

11 If $d = -11$, $e = -5$ and $f = 9$ work out these.

a $d + e$ **b** $e - f$ **c** $f - d$ **d** $-f - d$

e $d + e - f$ **f** $d - (e + f)$ **g** $f - (e - d)$ **h** $e + f - (d - f)$

i $e + e + e + e$ **j** $7e$ **k** $2d + e$ **l** $2e - f$

POSITIVE AND NEGATIVE INTEGERS (MULTIPLYING AND DIVIDING)

Essential Exercises

1 Copy and complete this multiplication table.

×	−6	−4	−2	0	2	4	6
−6							
−4							
−2							
0							
2							
4							
6							

2 Work out:
  a 3×-5 **b** -7×-3 **c** ✓ 8×-2 **d** -5×9
  e -9×-7 **f** -2×6 **g** ✓ -6×-5 **h** 7×-4

3 If $a = 2$, $b = -3$, $c = -4$ work out:
  a ab **b** ac **c** cb **d** $2b$
  e $2c + a$ **f** $3a - b$ **g** b^2 **h** $-3c$

4 How many negative sevens make negative twenty-one?

5 Work out:
  a $-8 \div -2$ **b** $-14 \div -2$ **c** ✓ $-12 \div -4$ **d** $-16 \div -8$
  e $-25 \div -5$ **f** $-36 \div -9$ **g** $-42 \div -7$ **h** $-40 \div -10$

6 a Work out -9×-3.   **b** How many negative threes make twenty seven?

7 Work out:
  a $12 \div -3$ **b** $21 \div -7$ **c** ✓ $32 \div -8$ **d** $45 \div -5$ **e** $48 \div -6$

8 Work out:
  a $-15 \div 5$ **b** $-24 \div 3$ **c** ✓ $-28 \div 4$ **d** $-49 \div 7$ **e** $-50 \div 5$

9 Calculate:

    a -8×-5 **b** ✓ 6×-9 **c** 5×-7 **d** -4×-7

    e -9×3 **f** ✓ $-36 \div -6$ **g** $48 \div -8$ **h** $55 \div -11$

    i $-60 \div -5$ **j** $-84 \div 12$ **k** $(-2)^2$ **l** $(-5)^2$

    m $(-7)^2$ **n** -10^2 **o** $(-3)^2 \times -2$ **p** $-1 \times -2 \times -3$

10 🏠 Work out:

    a $(-2 + 5) \times -2$ **b** $3 \times (1 - -4)$ **c** $-1 \times (4 + -6)$

    d $(8 - -4) \div 6$ **e** $(-8 + -7) \div 3$ **f** $-2 \times 4 + -3$

11 If $x = 6$, $y = -3$, and $z = -8$ work out the value of:

    a xy **b** xz **c** zy **d** $2y$

    e $3z$ **f** $x - y$ **g** y^2 **h** $2y + 3z$

    i $x + 2y$ **j** $y - z$ **k** $3y + z$ **l** $x \div y$

12 Calculate:

    a -20×-30 **b** -2×40 **c** -100×7 **d** 22×-3

    e $-60 \div -5$ **f** $54 \div -6$ **g** $-100 \div -25$ **h** $-55 \div 11$

    i $(-11)^2$ **j** $(-2)^3$ **k** $-2 \times -3 \times -4$ **l** $-1 \times 2 \times -50$

    m -5×0.1 **n** 4×-0.01 **o** -6×-0.1 **p** -8×-0.01

13 If $a = 2$, $b = 4$, $c = 6$, $x = -1$, $y = -3$, $z = -6$ work out these.

    a by **b** $cy + b$ **c** $2cx$ **d** $ax - y$

    e $bx + z$ **f** $ay - x$ **g** abx **h** cxy

    i $z + y^2$ **j** x^3 **k** $ax - by$ **l** $bc \div y$

    m $(a + z) \times y$ **n** $a + zy$ **o** $(y - b) \times a$ **p** $(a + z)^2$

14 Use the values of a, b, c, x, y and z given in question **2** to make these.

    a -30 **b** 5 **c** 20 **d** -2

Try to find more than one way.

(side column) 1 + 8 10,000 ÷ 2/3 × + 8 43 ÷ 1 10,000 × 1 149 16

Essential Exercises

1 Copy and complete these factor trees so that you can write the starting numbers as a product of prime numbers.

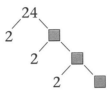

2 Copy and complete these tables for finding prime factors.
Write the numbers at the top of the tables as the product of primes.

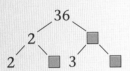

3 Choose your own method for writing these numbers as a product of primes.
  a 56   b 72   c ✓ 75   d 120   e 360

Use some of your answers to questions 1, 2 and 3 to answer the next four questions.

4 Find the HCF of these pairs.
  a 36 and 60   b ✓ 20 and 44   c 48 and 56   d 45 and 150

5 Find the LCM of these pairs.
  a 15 and 20   b ✓ 20 and 44   c 24 and 72   d 20 and 45

6 By writing each number as a product of primes find the HCF of these pairs.

   a 28 and 84   **b** 30 and 54   **c** 18 and 63   **d** 88 and 220

7 By writing each number as a product of primes find the LCM of these pairs.

   a 12 and 15   **b** 18 and 30   **c** 16 and 24   **d** 22 and 40

Consolidation Exercises

8 🏠 Find the HCF of these pairs.

   a 64 and 160   **b** ✓ 36 and 90   **c** 60 and 72   **d** 56 and 70

9 Find the LCM of these pairs.

   a 36 and 60   **b** ✓ 22 and 55   **c** 45 and 75   **d** 24 and 56

10 **a** Write down the value of A if $22 = 2 \times A$.

   b Write down the value of B if $35 = 7 \times B$.

   c Find the value of $A \times B$ (AB).

   d Show how to use these answers to work out 22×35.

11 Use factors to simplify and work out these products.

   a 32×75 **b** 18×15

Challenging Exercises

12 Find the LCM of these sets.

   a 8, 10 and 16   **b** 6, 15 and 45

13 Find the HCF of these sets.

   a 16, 32 and 80   **b** 36, 54 and 108

14 Use factors to simplify and work out these square roots.

   a $\sqrt{784}$ **b** $\sqrt{1024}$ **c** $\sqrt{1296}$

15 🏠 Simplify these fractions by cancelling.

   a $\frac{56}{84}$ **b** $\frac{96}{120}$ **c** $\frac{108}{240}$

POWERS AND ROOTS

Essential Exercises

1 What is the tenth cube number?

2 ✓ From the set of numbers below write down any which are:
a square numbers **b** cube numbers
c both a square number and a cube number.

   1   6   8   25   27   50   64   81

3 The positive square root of 20 ($\sqrt{20}$) is between two consecutive integers. Find them.

4 What is the nearest integer to $\sqrt{50}$?

5 Calculate the difference between the two square roots of 36.

6 Work out $2^3 + 3^3$.

7 Calculate:
a 4^3 **b** 0.4^3 **c** 40^3 **d** -4^3

8 Find:
a $\sqrt[3]{27}$ **b** $\sqrt[3]{1000}$ **c** $\sqrt[3]{27\,000}$

9 Work out:
a ✓ 2^5 **b** 3^4 **c** 10^6 **d** 1^7

10 ▦ Use a calculator to find these.
a 2.3^2 **b** 5.8^2 **c** 6.7^2 **d** 3.4^3

11 ▦ Use a calculator to find these correct to two decimal places.
a ✓ $\sqrt{8}$ **b** $\sqrt{30}$ **c** $\sqrt{44}$ **d** $\sqrt{78}$

12 Find the difference between 2^5 and 5^2.

13 Calculate:
a $(-5)^3$ **b** 0.6^2 **c** 20^3

14 Use this statement to find the two consecutive integers whose squares are nearest to 50. $\sqrt{49} < \sqrt{50} < \sqrt{64}$

15 Write a similar statement for each of these square roots and then find the two consecutive integers nearest to them.

    a ✓ $\sqrt{30}$ **b** $\sqrt{75}$ **c** $\sqrt{90}$

16 Write down the value of a and of b in the following statement and then the value of $\sqrt{3600}$.

$$\sqrt{3600} = \sqrt{(36 \times 100)} = \sqrt{(a^2 \times b^2)} = \sqrt{a^2} \times \sqrt{b^2} = a \times b = \blacksquare$$

17 Use factorisation to work out these.

    a $\sqrt{1600}$ **b** $\sqrt{484}$ **c** $\sqrt{576}$

18 Find the area of a square rug which measures 2.8 m along each side.

19 Find the volume of a cubical die of edge 2.3 cm correct to two decimal places.

Challenging Exercises

20 What is the next number in this sequence? 2, 9, 28, 65, ...

21 Write down the nearest integer to these cube roots.

    a $\sqrt[3]{10}$ **b** $\sqrt[3]{25}$ **c** $\sqrt[3]{999}$

22 Find the difference between:

    a $(5 + 2)^2$ and $5^2 + 2^2$ **b** $(3 + 8)^2$ and $3^2 + 8^2$ **c** $(4 + 7)^2$ and $4^2 + 7^2$

    Try to relate the differences to the starting numbers and explain the connections. (A diagram may help.)

23 Find the square root of: $2 \times (2^2 + 3^2) - 1$ without a calculator.

24   **a** Find the sum of the first five cube numbers.

    b Find the square of the sum of the first five integers.

    c What do you notice about your answers?

COMPARING FRACTIONS AND DECIMALS

8

1 Change these decimals to fractions in their lowest terms.

    a 0.549   **b** 0.456   **c** ✓ 0.675   **d** 0.875

    e 0.644   **f** 0.375   **g** 0.525   **h** 0.832

2 Use short division to change these fractions to decimals.

    a $\frac{5}{8}$ **b** $\frac{6}{5}$ **c** ✓ $\frac{19}{5}$ **d** $\frac{27}{8}$

3 Write these fractions as recurring decimals.

    a $\frac{1}{3}$ **b** $\frac{2}{9}$ **c** $\frac{5}{11}$ **d** $\frac{8}{11}$

    e $\frac{7}{3}$ **f** $\frac{11}{6}$ **g** $\frac{14}{9}$ **h** $\frac{37}{11}$

4 Use a calculator to change these fractions to decimals correct to 2 d.p.

    a $\frac{3}{13}$ **b** $\frac{12}{19}$ **c** ✓ $\frac{9}{17}$ **d** $\frac{16}{21}$

    e $\frac{25}{43}$ **f** $\frac{29}{13}$ **g** $\frac{38}{17}$ **h** $\frac{57}{23}$

5 Mark these fractions on the number line below.

    a $\frac{3}{5}$ **b** $\frac{14}{20}$ **c** $\frac{45}{50}$ **d** $\frac{9}{12}$

```
|    |    |    |    |    |    |    |    |    |    |
0   0.1  0.2  0.3  0.4  0.5  0.6  0.7  0.8  0.9   1
```

6 Change these fractions to twentieths and then write each set in order starting with the smallest.

    a ✓ $\frac{3}{4}, \frac{7}{10}, \frac{4}{5}$ **b** $\frac{2}{5}, \frac{7}{20}, \frac{1}{2}, \frac{3}{10}$

7 Change these fractions to hundredths and then write them in order starting with the largest.

    $\frac{1}{5}, \frac{1}{4}, \frac{3}{10}, \frac{13}{50}, \frac{7}{25}$

8 Find which is larger in each pair by changing the fractions to decimals.

    a $\frac{1}{3}$ $\frac{2}{5}$ **b** $\frac{3}{4}$ $\frac{7}{10}$

9 Copy these and put > or < between.

    a $\frac{3}{8}$ $\frac{2}{5}$ **b** $\frac{4}{9}$ $\frac{9}{20}$

10 Write this list in order starting with the smallest.

    $\frac{2}{5}, \frac{1}{3},$ 0.2, 0.33, $\frac{3}{10}$

11 Mark these fractions on the number line below.

a $\frac{31}{100}$ b $\frac{7}{20}$ c $\frac{19}{50}$ d $\frac{9}{25}$

e $\frac{1}{3}$ f $\frac{3}{8}$ g $\frac{4}{11}$ h $\frac{4}{13}$

```
|      |      |      |      |      |      |      |      |      |      |
0.30  0.31   0.32   0.33   0.34   0.35   0.36   0.37   0.38   0.39   0.4
```

12 Write these fractions first as recurring decimals and then correct to 2 d.p.

a $\frac{2}{11}$ b $\frac{5}{6}$ c ✓ $\frac{7}{9}$ d $\frac{2}{3}$

e ✓ $\frac{8}{3}$ f $\frac{19}{6}$ g $\frac{29}{9}$ h $\frac{100}{11}$

13 Work out the fraction halfway between these pairs.

a $\frac{2}{3}$ and $\frac{4}{5}$ b $\frac{1}{12}$ and $\frac{3}{4}$ c $\frac{4}{9}$ and $\frac{5}{6}$

14 Copy these and put > or < between.

a $\frac{11}{20}$ 0.52   b 0.33 $\frac{1}{3}$ c $\frac{5}{12}$ 0.42

15 🏠 Change these fractions to decimals and then write them in order starting with the smallest.

$$\frac{4}{9}, \frac{9}{20}, \frac{2}{5}, \frac{21}{50}, \frac{3}{7}$$

16 Write these fractions as decimals correct to 1 d.p.

a $\frac{2}{11}$ b $\frac{5}{9}$ c $\frac{17}{25}$ d $\frac{39}{50}$

17 These are Sam's marks in his last four maths tests.

$$\frac{5}{8}, \ \frac{6}{10}, \ 62\%, \ \frac{13}{20}$$

a What was his highest mark?   b What was his lowest mark?

18 a Use short division to work out $\frac{1}{7}$ as a decimal correct to 12 decimal places.

b Repeat a for $\frac{2}{7}, \frac{3}{7}, \frac{4}{7}, \frac{5}{7}$ and $\frac{6}{7}$.

c In addition to the fact that they are all recurring decimals what else do all your answers have in common?

ADDING AND SUBTRACTING FRACTIONS

Essential Exercises

Remember to give all answers in their lowest terms.

Work out the questions below and then check your answers with a calculator.

1 a $\frac{1}{3} + \frac{1}{2}$ b $\frac{1}{4} + \frac{1}{3}$ c $\frac{1}{5} + \frac{1}{2}$ d $\frac{1}{2} + \frac{1}{8}$

2 a $\frac{2}{5} + \frac{1}{4}$ b $\frac{1}{2} + \frac{3}{7}$ c $\frac{2}{9} + \frac{1}{6}$ d $\frac{1}{5} + \frac{3}{10}$

3 a $\frac{3}{5} + \frac{2}{15}$ b ✓ $\frac{3}{8} + \frac{5}{12}$ c $\frac{3}{10} + \frac{2}{5}$ d $\frac{4}{9} + \frac{7}{18}$

4 a $\frac{3}{4} + \frac{3}{8}$ b $\frac{3}{5} + \frac{7}{10}$ c $\frac{7}{8} + \frac{1}{2}$ d $\frac{5}{6} + \frac{1}{3}$

   e $\frac{2}{3} + \frac{5}{12}$ f $\frac{5}{8} + \frac{7}{16}$ g $\frac{4}{5} + \frac{4}{15}$ h $\frac{2}{9} + \frac{5}{6}$

   i $\frac{2}{3} + \frac{3}{4}$ j ✓ $\frac{5}{6} + \frac{7}{9}$ k $\frac{7}{8} + \frac{3}{4}$ l $\frac{3}{4} + \frac{4}{5}$

5 a $\frac{1}{2} - \frac{1}{8}$ b $\frac{1}{3} - \frac{1}{4}$ c $\frac{1}{2} - \frac{1}{5}$ d $\frac{1}{6} - \frac{1}{9}$

   e $\frac{3}{4} - \frac{1}{8}$ f $\frac{7}{8} - \frac{1}{2}$ g $\frac{7}{9} - \frac{1}{3}$ h $\frac{7}{10} - \frac{1}{5}$

6 a $\frac{4}{5} - \frac{3}{10}$ b $\frac{7}{8} - \frac{3}{4}$ c $\frac{8}{9} - \frac{2}{3}$ d $\frac{9}{14} - \frac{2}{7}$

   e $\frac{5}{6} - \frac{2}{3}$ f ✓ $\frac{3}{4} - \frac{2}{3}$ g $\frac{5}{6} - \frac{7}{9}$ h $\frac{4}{5} - \frac{3}{4}$

7 At the pantomime $\frac{2}{5}$ of the audience were girls and $\frac{1}{4}$ were boys. The rest were adults.

   a What fraction of the audience was children?

   b What fraction was adults?

8 A school organised two visits for Year 8 pupils. If $\frac{3}{8}$ of the pupils chose to go swimming and $\frac{9}{16}$ chose to go ice skating what fraction did not go on a visit?

Consolidation Exercises

Work out these and then check your answers with a calculator.

9 🏠 **a** $\frac{5}{12} + \frac{1}{3} - \frac{1}{4}$ **b** $\frac{7}{15} + \frac{3}{5} - \frac{2}{3}$ **c** $\frac{7}{8} - \frac{1}{2} + \frac{3}{4}$

10 a $1\frac{1}{12} + \frac{1}{3}$ **b** $2\frac{5}{8} + \frac{1}{4}$ **c** $2\frac{1}{9} + \frac{5}{6}$
  d $1\frac{1}{4} + \frac{2}{3}$ **e** ✓ $3\frac{1}{5} + \frac{1}{2}$ **f** $\frac{2}{5} + 4\frac{1}{2}$

11 a $2\frac{3}{4} - \frac{1}{2}$ **b** ✓ $4\frac{7}{10} - \frac{2}{5}$ **c** $2\frac{11}{2} - \frac{5}{6}$
  d $1\frac{7}{9} - \frac{2}{3}$ **e** $3\frac{5}{6} - \frac{2}{3}$ **f** $5\frac{4}{5} - \frac{3}{10}$

12 👥 A boy spent $\frac{3}{4}$ hour on his geography homework and $\frac{2}{3}$ hour on his history homework. How long, in hours, did he spend doing both homework tasks?

13 👥 A journey consists of a $\frac{1}{5}$ hour taxi ride to the railway station, $2\frac{1}{2}$ hours on a train and a $\frac{3}{10}$ hour bus ride. How long, in hours did the journey last?

Challenging Exercises

14 a $\frac{3}{4} + \frac{4}{5} + \frac{7}{10}$ **b** $\frac{2}{3} + \frac{5}{8} + \frac{7}{12}$ **c** $\frac{1}{3} + \frac{3}{5} - \frac{2}{15}$ **d** $\frac{7}{8} - \frac{2}{3} + \frac{13}{24}$

15 The sum of three fractions is $1\frac{3}{4}$. If two of the fractions are $\frac{2}{3}$ and $\frac{5}{8}$ what is the third?

16 🏠 **a** Add the first four fractions in this list.

$$\frac{3}{10}, \quad \frac{3}{100}, \quad \frac{3}{1000}, \quad \frac{3}{10\,000}, \quad \frac{3}{100\,000}$$

  b Continue the list and add the first seven fractions.
  c Write your answers to **a** and **b** as a decimal.
  d 👥 If you could continue the list 'for ever' and add all the fractions what would the total be? Give your answer as a decimal and as a fraction.

17 What would be the total if this list: $\frac{1}{2} + \frac{1}{4} + \frac{1}{8} + \frac{1}{16} + \dots$ were continued 'for ever' and all the fractions added together?

1
+
8
10,000
÷
2/3
×
+
8
43
÷
1
10,000
×
1
4
9
16

MULTIPLYING AND DIVIDING INTEGERS AND FRACTIONS

Essential Exercises

1 Work out:

  a $\frac{1}{8} \times 5$ **b** ✓ $\frac{2}{5} \times 2$ **c** $\frac{3}{7} \times 4$ **d** $10 \times \frac{2}{3}$

2 Work out:

  a $\frac{2}{3}$ of 10   **b** $\frac{3}{5}$ of 11   **c** ✓ $\frac{3}{4}$ of £90   **d** $\frac{5}{8}$ of 60 yards

3 Which is the odd one out in each set?

  a $\frac{5}{8}$ of 11, $\frac{5}{8} \times 11$, $5 \times 11 \div 8$, $5 \div 11 \times 8$

  b $\frac{4}{9} \times 16$, $\frac{16}{9} \times 4$, $\frac{9}{4} \times 16$, $\frac{4}{9}$ of 16

4 Simplify these by cancelling and write the answers as mixed numbers.

  a $\frac{3}{14} \times \frac{49}{1}$ **b** ✓ $\frac{7}{36} \times \frac{48}{1}$

5 True or false?

  a $\frac{2}{3} = 2 \div 3$ **b** $5 \times \frac{3}{4} > 5$ **c** $3 \div 8 = 3 \times \frac{1}{8}$ **d** $2 \div \frac{9}{10} > 2$

6 How many thirds are there in fifteen?

7 **a** $12 \div \frac{1}{3}$ **b** $12 \div \frac{2}{3}$ **c** $6 \div \frac{3}{4}$ **d** $8 \div \frac{2}{5}$

8 Jack spent $\frac{2}{5}$ of his pocket money on sweets and $\frac{3}{8}$ on a magazine. He saved the remainder.

  a What fraction of his money did he spend?

  b What fraction was left?

  c If he was given £2.40 last week how much did he save?

9 The birthday cake for my grandmother had 96 candles. If $\frac{5}{8}$ were white, $\frac{1}{3}$ were red and the rest blue how many blue candles were there?

1 + 8 10,000 ÷ 2/3 × + 8 43 ÷ 1 10,000 × 1 4 9 16

Consolidation Exercises

10 Work out:

    a $\frac{3}{4} \times 5$
    b $5 \times \frac{7}{8}$
    c $\frac{7}{20} \times 7$
    d $\frac{2}{11} \times 9$

11 Work out using cancelling to simplify:

    a $\frac{7}{12}$ of 54
    b ✓ $\frac{8}{15}$ of 35
    c $\frac{9}{20}$ of 45
    d $\frac{11}{25}$ of 55

12 Work out:

    a $6 \div \frac{1}{5}$
    b $6 \div \frac{2}{5}$
    c $6 \div \frac{3}{5}$
    d $8 \div \frac{1}{3}$

    e $8 \div \frac{2}{3}$
    f ✓ $9 \div \frac{3}{4}$
    g $10 \div \frac{2}{5}$
    h $12 \div \frac{4}{5}$

13 🏠 There are two equal pairs in this list. Find them and then write down the value of the odd one out.

> $\frac{7}{9}$ of 63, $63 \div (9 \times 7)$, $\frac{9}{7} \times 63$, $9 \times 63 \div 7$, $\frac{63}{9}$ of 7

Challenging Exercises

14 Work out:

    a $3 \div \frac{2}{5}$
    b $2 \div \frac{4}{5}$
    c $4 \div \frac{3}{4}$
    d $\frac{3}{4} \div 4$

15 How many times can $\frac{3}{5}$ be subtracted from 6?

16 Calculate:

    a $(\frac{4}{5} - \frac{3}{4}) \times 8$
    b $5 \div (\frac{1}{3} + \frac{2}{9})$
    c $(\frac{11}{12} - \frac{5}{6}) \times 3$

17 🔲 🏠 Lorena ate $\frac{5}{11}$ of her sweets and gave half of those that were left to her sister. What fraction of her sweets were left?

18 **a** Work out $5 \div \frac{3}{2}$

    b Find $5 \div 1\frac{1}{2}$

    c Calculate $3 \div 2\frac{1}{2}$

19 Calculate:

    a $\frac{3}{5} \div 2$
    b $\frac{4}{3} \div 5$
    c $2\frac{1}{4} \div 3$

Side bar (left margin): 1 + 8 10,000 ÷ 2/3 × + 8 43 ÷ 1 10,000 × 1 4 9 16

CONVERTING FRACTIONS, DECIMALS AND PERCENTAGES

Essential Exercises

1 Change these percentages to fractions in their lowest terms.

   a 85%   **b** ✓ 32%   **c** 54%   **d** 120%

2 Change these fractions to percentages.

   a $\frac{13}{20}$ **b** $\frac{17}{25}$ **c** ✓ $\frac{41}{50}$ **d** $1\frac{1}{2}$

3 🖩 Use a calculator to change these fractions to percentages correct to 1 d.p.

   a $\frac{5}{6}$ **b** $\frac{4}{7}$ **c** ✓ $\frac{6}{11}$ **d** $2\frac{2}{3}$

4 Change these decimals to percentages.

   a 0.29   **b** ✓ 0.7   **c** 0.03   **d** 1.3

5 The probability that it rains on Sports Day is 0.39. Write this as a percentage.

6 A farm shop sold 200 eggs last Saturday. Of these, 62 were brown eggs. What percentage of the eggs sold were brown?

7 In a school, two children out of every five go home for lunch. What percentage stay at school during lunchtime?

8 This pie chart shows the choices of the children who bought a school lunch.

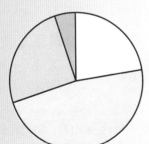

   ☐ Today's Special

   ☐ Beans and chips

   ☐ Salad

   ☐ Sandwiches

Estimate the percentage of children who chose each option.

9 🏠 Carry out a survey of twenty people in Year 8 to find out which of these four choices they prefer for lunch. Use your results to calculate the percentage who choose each option. Draw a pie chart to illustrate your findings.

10 Change these percentages to mixed numbers.

    a 115%   **b** ✓ 350%

11 Change these fractions to percentages.

    a $\frac{9}{4}$ **b** $\frac{16}{3}$

12 Change these decimals to percentages.

    a 1.53   **b** ✓ 2.09

13 Seven-eighths of the children in Class 8X are going on a field trip. What percentage is this?

14 A town council spends 36% of its budget on education. What fraction is this?

15 Try to find out what percentage of the budget your local council spends on education.

Challenging Exercises

16 Change these percentages to fractions in their lowest terms.

    a $12\frac{1}{2}$%   **b** $7\frac{1}{2}$%   **c** $133\frac{1}{3}$%

17 Change these fractions to percentages correct to 1 d.p.

    a $\frac{19}{12}$ **b** $\frac{38}{15}$

18 Change these decimals to percentages.

    a 0.457   **b** 1.275

19 The probability that Anya goes shopping on Saturdays is 40%. Write this as a fraction. How many Saturdays in the next ten weeks do you expect Anya to go shopping?

20 Mrs Lowe spends $\frac{2}{5}$ of her earnings on food, 12% on clothes and cosmetics, 0.35 on rent, and 8% on entertainment. She saves the rest. What percentage of her earnings does she save?

1
+
8
10,000 ÷
2/3
×
+
8
43
÷
1
10,000
×
1
4
9
16

WORKING WITH PERCENTAGES

Essential Exercises

Use mental methods for questions 1–4.

1 Find:
    a 55% of 80   **b** 12% of 300   **c** 110% of 90

2 Work out:
    a 1% of 130   **b** ✓ 7% of 130   **c** 107% of 130

3 Work out:
    a 1% of 29   **b** 4% of 29   **c** 104% of 29

4 Calculate:
    a 31% of 11   **b** ✓ 21% of 9   **c** 17% of 7
    d 22% of 4 m   **e** 9% of 120 ml   **f** 11% of 350 g

5 Write down a decimal calculation and use a calculator to work out these correct to 2 d.p.
    a 17% of 61   **b** 23% of 44   **c** 27% of 58
    d 47% of 85 kg   **e** 73% of 39 m   **f** 94% of 164 g

6 Use a calculator to work out these correct to the nearest penny.
    a 13% of £14   **b** 27% of £53   **c** 44% of £74

7 A meat pie label claims that 45% of the total weight is real meat. If the pie weighs 740 g what is the weight of the meat it contains?

8 There are 180 children in Year 8 in a school and 15% of them are going on a French exchange visit. How many of the children are going to France?

9 Some more Year 8 children are going on an 11-day exchange trip to Germany. The weather forecast says that during the period of their visit the probability of rain is about 18%. How many wet days should they expect?

10 In a book containing 400 pages there are errors on 8 pages. What percentage of the pages have errors?

Consolidation Exercises

Use mental methods for questions 1 and 2.

11 Find:

    a 11% of 65 kg   **b** 60% of 140 cm   **c** 110% of 120

12 Work out:

    a 7% of 52 m   **b** ✓ 12% of 36 g   **c** 112% of 36 g

13 🖩 Write down a decimal calculation and use a calculator to work out:

    a 71% of 64   **b** ✓ 87% of £273   **c** 135% of 85 tonnes

14 🔲 John saved £26 for his holidays and Louise saved £21. John spent 19% of his money on ice-cream and Louise spent 23% of hers on ice-cream. Who spent the most money on ice-cream and by how much?

15 🔲 🏠 **a** In a rose garden, which has 150 rose bushes, 30% have pink roses. How many bushes have pink roses?

    b One bush has 25 roses. Four are picked to make buttonholes. What percentage are picked?

Challenging Exercises

16 🖩 Write down a decimal calculation and use a calculator to work out these correct to 1 d.p.

    a 46.3% of 78   **b** 123% of 863   **c** 117.5% of 35

17 🖩 Work out correct to the nearest penny:

    a 63% of £25.80   **b** 38% of £36.75   **c** 14% of £5.70

18 🔲 🏠 The label on a 4-pint bottle of semi-skimmed milk has the following information:

> 'This bottle contains 2.272 litres of milk' and 'Only 1.4% fat'.

How many millilitres of fat does the milk contain, correct to 1 d.p.?

PERCENTAGE CHANGE

Essential Exercises

1 True or false? Explain.

   a An increase of 200% is equivalent to 'doubling'.

   b If a car decreases its value by 50% it is worth half its original value.

   c A plant that grows to six times its original height has increased its height by 500%.

   d A price reduction of 25% means that a 'new' price is three-quarters of an 'old' price.

   e A man loses 5% of his weight one month and then increases his weight by 5% in the next so he weighs the same as he did to start with.

2 Use mental methods to work out these:

   a increase 80 by 25%   **b** ✓ increase 60 by 20%   **c** increase 50 by 200%

   d decrease 90 by 10%   **e** decrease 70 by 50%   **f** decrease 12 by 100%

3 🖩 Use a calculator to work out the new values after these changes:

   a an increase of 13% on 64   **b** ✓ an increase of 42% on 78 kg

   c a decrease of 9% on 57   **d** a decrease of 22% on 67 m

   e an increase of 4% on £765   **f** a decrease of 79% on £36

   g an increase of 105% on 38   **h** an increase of 230% on £48.

4 In a sale prices are reduced by 30%. Work out the sale prices of these items.

	Item	Original price
a	Coat	£60
b	Shoes	£35
c ✓	Book	£16
d	Television	£380

5 💡 Paul has saved £120 in his bank account. How much interest will he get after one year if the rate of interest is 4% p.a. (p.a. = per annum)?

6 💡 Gemma borrows £650 from the bank. The interest on this loan is 3% p.a. She decides to pay back the loan at the end of the first year. How much does she have to pay back altogether?

Consolidation Exercises

7  Use a calculator to work out the new values, correct to 2 d.p., after these changes.

    a an increase of 43% on 86   **b** ✓ a decrease of 4% on 374

    c an increase of 23.8% on 87   **d** a decrease of 44.5% on £38

8 The following list shows the prices of some items before VAT (Value Added Tax) at 17.5% has been added. Calculate the final price of each item to the nearest penny.

	Item	Price without VAT
a	electric drill	£65
b ✓	microwave	£89
c	settee	£395

9 If Mr Frost pays cash for the new car he wants it will cost £8795. He could instead pay a deposit of 20% and monthly instalments of £309.50 for 2 years. How much does he save on the purchase if he pays the cash price?

Challenging Exercises

10 The price of a bicycle before VAT at 17.5% has been added is £126. Show how to calculate the amount of VAT without using a calculator.

11 A girl scored 75 marks in a Maths test at the end of Year 7. In Year 8 her score rose by 20% but in Year 9 it fell by 20%. What did she score in Year 9?

12 Find the value of these investments after one year.

	Investment	Rate of interest p.a. (p.a. = per annum)
a	£2750	6%
b	£38 500	7%
c	£3000	$4\frac{1}{2}$%

USING DIRECT PROPORTION

Essential Exercises

1 Here are some exchange rates.

> £1 = 1.50 euros (in France)
> £1 = 11 kroner (in Norway)
> £1 = 2.2 francs (in Switzerland)
> £1 = 3 dollars (in New Zealand)
> £1 = 15 rands (in South Africa)

Work out the value of:

a £20 in euros   **b** £8 in rands   **c** £250 in dollars
d 132 kroner in £   **e** 12 euros in £   **f** 66 francs in £.

g For her holiday in France, Yasmin changed £60 into euros. She spent 75 euros and changed the remainder into £ on her return. How much money in £ did she receive?

2 ✓ If twelve pencils cost 72p find the cost of seven pencils.

3 If three CDs cost £39 find the cost of seven CDs.

4 A car goes 80 miles on two gallons of petrol. How far can it go on 5 gallons?

5 Two cakes take 3 hours to cook in a large oven. How long does it take for three cakes to cook?

6 A cake recipe for eight people uses 3 eggs and 160 g of sugar.
a ✓ How many eggs would be needed to make a similar cake for sixteen people?
b How much sugar would be needed to make a similar cake for twelve people?

7 A man earns £40 for an eight-hour shift.
a How much does he earn in 5 hours?
b How many hours does he work in order to earn £65?

Consolidation Exercises

8 Use the information on exchange rates from question **1** to work out the value of £10 in dollars and $150 in pounds. Use these values to draw a graph to convert pounds and dollars.
Use your graph to convert:
  a £44 to dollars   **b** $105 to pounds.

9 ✓ A plan of a garden is drawn using a scale of 1 cm to 50 cm.
  a A flower border is 3 m wide and 12 m long. What lengths on the plan represent these measurements?
  b On the plan a lawn is 20 cm long. How long is the real lawn?

10 🏠 A map of London uses a scale of 1 : 10 000.
  a On the map the distance from Buckingham Palace to Westminster Abbey is 9 cm. How far is it to walk?
  b The distance from the British Museum to the Tower of London is about 4 km. How far is this on the map?

Challenging Exercises

11 Two boy scouts take 20 minutes to clean a car. How long does it take five scouts?

12 🏠 Pecks and bushels are old Imperial units once used for measuring amounts of cereals. Given that 2 gallons = 1 peck and 4 pecks = 1 bushel, find:
  a 12 gallons in pecks   **b** 36 pecks in bushels
  c 16 gallons in bushels   **d** 20 bushels in gallons.

SIMPLIFYING RATIOS

Essential Exercises

1 Simplify the following ratios by cancelling.
   a 14 : 21   **b** 25 : 75   **c** 35 : 50
   d 32 : 72   **e** 24 : 40   **f** 180 : 270

2 Copy and complete:
   a 6 : 30 = 1 : ■   **b** 20 : 60 = 1 : ■
   c ✓ 36 : 9 = ■ : 1   **d** 60 : 12 = ■ : 1

3 Simplify the following ratios.
   a 50p : £3   **b** ✓ 80p : £3.20   **c** 75p : £2.50
   d 30 cm : 1 m   **e** 2 m : 40 cm   **f** 8 mm : 4 cm
   g 0.8 cm : 24 mm   **h** ✓ 4 m : 120 cm   **i** 2.5 kg : 500 g
   j 700 g : 1 kg   **k** 750 g : 3 kg   **l** 350 mm : 7m

4 A bookmark is 16 cm long and 30 mm wide.
   a What is the ratio of the length to the width?
   b What is the ratio of the length to the perimeter?

5 Two of the angles in a triangle are 40° and 60°.
   a Calculate the third angle.
   b What is the ratio of the smallest angle to the largest angle?

6 Andrew is 12 years old. He has a younger brother, Ben, aged 8 years and an older brother, Mike, aged 16 years.
   a Write down and simplify the ratio of Andrew's age : Ben's age : Mike's age.
   b What proportion is Andrew's age of the total of their ages?

7 The scores of three children in a game are 45, 60 and 75.
   a Write down and simplify the ratio of the scores.
   b What fraction is the lowest score of the highest score?

Consolidation Exercises

8 Copy and complete:
- **a** $45 : 15 = \blacksquare : 1$
- **b** ✓ $10 : 7 = 1 : \blacksquare$
- **c** $0.2 : 2 = 0.1 : \blacksquare = 1 : \blacksquare$

9 Simplify these ratios:
- **a** $2 : 6 : 10$
- **b** $5 : 15 : 20$
- **c** $12 : 18 : 36$
- **d** $9 : 90 : 180$
- **e** ✓ $60p : 80p : £1$
- **f** $25\,cm : 50\,cm : 2\,m$

10 In a jar of sweets the ratio of the number of red sweets to green sweets to yellow sweets is $8 : 16 : 40$.
- **a** Simplify this ratio.
- **b** What fraction of the sweets are yellow?
- **c** What percentage of the sweets are green?

Challenging Exercises

11 Copy and complete:
- **a** $3 : 2 = \blacksquare : 1$
- **b** $60 : 24 = \blacksquare : 2 = \blacksquare : 1$
- **c** $80 : 100 = 1 : \blacksquare$

12 Simplify these ratios:
- **a** $75p : £1.50 : £3$
- **b** $80\,mm : 2.4\,cm : 40\,cm$
- **c** $750\,g : 2\,kg : 1.5\,kg$
- **d** $400\,mm : 80\,cm : 1.2\,m$
- **e** 9 inches : 2 feet : 1 yard.

13 In an isosceles triangle one of the base angles is 75°.
- **a** Calculate the size of the third angle.
- **b** What is the ratio of the third angle to the angle sum?
- **c** Write down and simplify a ratio of all three angles.

14 Kathryn is twelve years old. She has twin cousins, Jessie and Ruth.
- **a** If the ratio of Kathryn's age to Jessie's age, in its simplest form, is $4 : 5$ how old is Jessie?
- **b** Write down in its simplest form the ratio of Jessie's age : Ruth's age.

The vertical bar on the left contains: 1 + 8 10,000 ÷ 2/3 × + 8 43 ÷ 1 10,000 × 1 4 9 16

DIVIDING IN A GIVEN RATIO 8

Essential Exercises

1 Divide 45p in the ratio 1 : 4.

2 ✓ Divide £28 in the ratio 3 : 4.

3 Divide 220m in the ratio 3 : 8.

4 Divide 90 cm in the ratio 2 : 3 : 4.

5 ✓ Mrs White has fifteen grandchildren. The ratio of the number of grandsons to the number of granddaughters is 2 : 3. How many granddaughters does she have?

6 In a tray of eggs the ratio of the number of white eggs to the number of brown eggs is 3 : 7. If the tray contains 150 eggs how many are brown?

Consolidation Exercises

7 At a party the ratio of the numbers of girls, boys and adults is 9 : 10 : 1. If there are sixty people at the party how many of them are girls? What percentage are adults?

8 ✓ In a class the ratio of the numbers of boys and girls is 2 : 3. If there are 10 boys how many pupils are there in the class?

Challenging Exercises

9 The ratio of the angles of a triangle in its simplest form is 2 : 2 : 5.
   a What type of triangle is it?
   b Calculate the size of each angle?

10 A rectangle is five times as long as it is wide. What is the ratio of its length to its perimeter?

11 In a packet of 100 balloons the ratio of the numbers of red, blue, and yellow balloons is 2 : 3 : 5. How many balloons of each colour are there? If five of each colour burst, find and simplify the ratio of the numbers of each colour remaining.

USING POWERS OF TEN

Essential Exercises

1 Calculate:
  a $0.28 \times 10\,000$ **b** $703 \times 100\,000$ **c** ✓ $65 \div 10\,000$ **d** $0.78 \div 100$
  e 5.9×0.1 **f** 27.3×0.01 **g** ✓ $1.94 \div 0.1$ **h** $0.741 \div 0.01$

2 **a** How many bytes are there in a megabyte?
  b How many micrograms are there in 10 grams?

3 Write the value of these in figures.
  a 1.6×10^6 **b** ✓ 70×10^0 **c** 0.3×10^3 **d** 3200×10^1

4 Write these as fractions in their lowest terms and as decimals.
  a 3×10^{-1} **b** 5×10^{-2} **c** ✓ 4×10^{-1}

5 Convert these measurements to the units given in brackets.
  a $2.8\,kg$ (g) **b** $760\,mg$ (g) **c** $6.4\,km$ (cm)

Consolidation Exercises

6 Convert these volumes to the units stated in brackets.
  a $8.4\,cm^3$ (mm^3) **b** ✓ $1200\,mm^3$ (cm^3)
  c $9.542\,m^3$ (cm^3) **d** $2\,m^3$ (mm^3)

7 🏠 **a** How many micrometres are there in 4 metres?
  b Change 10 metres to nanometres. **c** What is 60 metres in picometres?

Challenging Exercises

8 Work out the volume of a cuboid with length 2.5 m, width 24 cm and thickness 8 mm. Give your answer in mm^3. What object might have these measurements?

9 🏠 **a** Change 7000 micrometres to metres.
  b Change 2 million nanometres to metres.

STANDARD FORM 9

Essential Exercises

1 Copy and complete these with decimal numbers as answers.

a $3 \times 10^{-2} = 3 \times \frac{1}{\blacksquare} = 3 \div 100 = \blacksquare$ b $6.5 \times 10^{-2} = 6.5 \div \blacksquare = \blacksquare$

c $7 \times 10^{-3} = 7 \times \frac{1}{\blacksquare} = 7 \blacksquare 1000 = \blacksquare$ d $2.4 \times 10^{-3} = 2.4 \blacksquare 000 = \blacksquare$

2 Find the value of these:

a 24.1×10^3 b ✓ $56\,400 \div 10^4$ c $34.8 \div 10^3$

d 0.86×10^4 e $72\,300 \div 10^3$ f ✓ 0.00643×10^4

g $6407 \div 10^5$ h $0.000\,704 \times 10^5$

3 Write these as ordinary numbers.

a ✓ 6.3×10^3 b 2.42×10^4 c 1.965×10^5 d 8.476×10^9

e 3.25×10^6 f 5.03×10^4 g 4×10^{10} h $3.000\,9 \times 10^7$

4 Write down the value of A in each of these.

a ✓ $4\,000 = 4 \times 10^A$ b $35\,600 = 3.5 \times 10^A$ c $298\,000 = 2.98 \times 10^A$

d $24.7 = 2.47 \times 10^A$ e $641.8 = A \times 10^2$ f $6070 = A \times 10^3$

5 Write these as ordinary numbers.

a $6 \div 10^2$ b $2.45 \div 10^2$ c $3.205 \div 10^5$ d $9.060\,5 \div 10^9$

6 Write down the value of A in each of these.

a $0.32 = 3.2 \div 10^A$ b $0.007 = 7 \div 10^A$

c $0.053 = A \div 10^2$ d $0.000\,5 = 5 \div 10^A$

7 Write these as ordinary numbers.

a 3.65×10^5 b $7.04 \div 10^2$ c $2.37 \div 10^4$ d 6.0303×10^3

8 There are about 31.5 million seconds in a year.

a This number can be written as 3.15×10^n. What is the value of n?

b Work out the number of seconds in a century and write your answer in a similar way. (Ignore leap years.)

9 a The Earth was formed about four and a half billion years ago. This number can be written as 4.5×10^n. What is the value of n?

b The oldest fossils suggest that life on Earth began about 3.5×10^9 years ago. How old was the Earth when this happened?

10 Write these as decimal numbers.

   a 3.7×10^{-1} **b** ✓ 1.38×10^{-2} **c** 4.97×10^{-1} **d** 5.1×10^{-2}

11 Write these numbers in standard form.

   a ✓ 8640   **b** 5030   **c** 34 000   **d** 0.641   **e** 0.038

12 The following table shows information about the composition of human blood, using ordinary numbers and numbers in standard form.

Component	Number in average adult human		Size (in mm)	
Red blood cells	2.6×10^{13}	_____	1.07×10^{-2}	_____
White blood cells Type 1	_____	25 000 000 000	_____	0.012
Type 2	2.4×10^{8}	_____	1.47×10^{-2}	_____
Platelets	_____	275 000 000 000	_____	0.0023

   a 🏠 List the components in order of size, with their size as decimal numbers, starting with the smallest.

   b 📱 Are there more Type 1 or Type 2 white blood cells? About how many times as many?

13 Write these numbers in standard form.

   a 493 000   **b** 60 500   **c** 300 700   **d** 0.085 3   **e** 0.003 02

14 Write these as ordinary numbers.

   a 4.03×10^{6} **b** 1.694×10^{5} **c** 6.001×10^{1} **d** 3.8×10^{-3} **e** 5.08×10^{-4}

15 📱 Using the table in question **12**:

   a Find the total of Type 1 and Type 2 white blood cells.

   b About how many times more red blood cells than white blood cells are there?

16 📱 🏠 A googol is 10^{100}. How many zeros are there in twenty googols?

ROUNDING

Essential Exercises

1 Round these to the nearest whole number.

   a 5.870 5   **b** ✓ 2.098   **c** 14.480 7

   d 0.708   **e** 29.890 1   **f** 0.276

2 Round these to 1 decimal place (1 d.p.).

   a 7.329 8   **b** ✓ 4.029   **c** 3.692 1

   d 12.387   **e** 0.650 2   **f** 2.983 5

3 Round these to 2 decimal places (2 d.p.).

   a 7.231 6   **b** ✓ 1.639   **c** 3.050 9

   d 5.296 3   **e** 0.057 3   **f** 6.003 2

4 In **a–c** below round these to: **i** the nearest whole number **ii** 1 decimal place (1 d.p.) **iii** 2 decimal places (2 d.p.).

   a 8.426 1   **b** 7.906 9   **c** 5.959 52

5 Round these to the number of decimal places shown in brackets.

   a 3.908 7 (2)   **b** 0.740 9 (2)   **c** 32.863 (1)

   d 1.093 7 (1)   **e** 4.984 (1)   **f** 4.697 8 (2)

6 Use a calculator to evaluate these and give your answer to the number of decimal places shown in brackets.

   a $57 \div 14$ (1)   **b** $482 \div 23$ (2)   **c** $2 \div 19$ (2)

   d 6.32×4.17 (1)   **e** $2.9 \div 0.74$ (1)   **f** 5.78^2 (2)

Consolidation Exercises

7 Round these numbers to one significant figure (1 s.f.).

   a 5632   **b** ✓ 0.058 2   **c** sixteen thousand

   d 49.398   **e** 40 976   **f** 0.000 925

8 Round these numbers to two significant figures (2 s.f.).

   a 30 875
   b ✓ 62 086
   c one hundred and nine thousand
   d 54.837
   e 6.085 2
   f 0.805 4

9 Round these numbers to three significant figures (3 s.f.).

   a 397 059
   b ✓ 53.937
   c two-thirds of a million
   d 2797
   e 5.299 7
   f 40.960 8

10 🏠 Round these numbers to the number of significant figures given in brackets.

   a 54.562 (3)
   b 3.756 (2)
   c 0.085 28 (1)
   d 30.542 (2)
   e 40 600 (1)
   f 239.97 (3)

11 Round these to 3 decimal places (3 d.p.).

   a 2.085 4
   b 7.380 5
   c 1.497 3
   d 3.259 7
   e 0.000 41
   f 4.299 51

Challenging Exercises

12 📱 First estimate and then use a calculator to evaluate these and give your answer correct to 3 s.f.

   a $349 \div 17$
   b $58 \div 31$
   c 537^2
   d 2.74^2
   e $(34 + 28) \times 79$
   f $(217 - 58) \div 46$

13 📱 🏠 Use a calculator to find, correct to 3 s.f.:

   a the area of a square of side 22.5 cm
   b the area of a rectangle 34.2 cm by 17.5 cm
   c the circumference of a circle of radius 8.4 cm
   d the hypotenuse of a right-angled triangle given that the other two sides are 6 cm and 7 cm.

(margin decoration) 1 + 8 10,000 ÷ 2/3 × + 8 43 ÷ 1 10,000 × 1 4 9 16

ESTIMATING

Essential Exercises

1 Round each of the numbers in these calculations to the nearest whole number and estimate the answers.
  a 9.86×3.28 **b** ✓ 6.29×8.73 **c** 10.86×5.37
  d $45.3 \div 8.7$ **e** $69.5 \div 9.83$ **f** ✓ 6.21^2

2 a 📱 Use a calculator to work out the answers to the calculations in question **1** and give your answers correct to 1 d.p.
  b Compare your answers to both questions and correct any errors you find.

3 📱 Find the area of these shapes correct to 1 d.p.
  a ✓ a rectangle 2.17 m by 7.86 m   **b** a rectangle 5.2 cm by 12.3 cm
  c a square of side 9.7 cm   **d** a square of side 3.8 cm
  e a circle of radius 7 cm   **f** a circle of diameter 10 cm

4 📱 Find the volume of cuboids with these measurements, correct to 2 d.p.
  a length 3.2 cm, width 4.3 cm, height 1.9 cm
  b length 6.8 cm, width 5.1 cm, height 9.7 cm
  c length 19.5 cm, width 10.3 cm , height 3.7 cm

5 Round each of these numbers to 1 d.p. or to the nearest 10 as appropriate and estimate the answers to these calculations.
  a 39.2×0.184 **b** $58.47 \div 5.986$ **c** 198.5×0.498

6 🏠 Which of the statements below uses an appropriate number of decimal places? Write down an improved statement for those which use an inappropriate number of decimal places.
  a The teacher's desk is 2.3726 m wide.
  b The mean height of the children is 1.43 m.
  c The distance to London is 165.348 miles.
  d The team's average goal score is 1.527 goals per match.
  e The tallest book on the shelf is 32.5 cm.

Consolidation Exercises

7 ✓ Mr Green wishes to pay £8000, to the nearest £1000, for a car. What is the price of the least expensive car he would buy?

8 The number of people at a recent 'Concert in the Park' was thirty thousand to the nearest thousand. Copy and complete this statement in which p represents the number of people at the concert.

■ ≤ p ≤ ■

9 The population of London is eight million to the nearest million. What are the least and greatest values of the population of London.

10 The population of Gibraltar is twenty-nine thousand to the nearest thousand. Copy and complete this statement in which p represents the population of Gibraltar.

■ ≤ p ≤ ■

11 A rectangular lawn is 36 m long and 24 m wide, to the nearest metre. Copy and complete these statements in which l represents the length of the room and w represents the width.

■ ≤ l < ■   ■ ≤ w < ■

12 A rectangular picture is 56 cm long and 32 cm wide, to the nearest centimetre. What is the least the perimeter could be?

Challenging Exercises

13 Round each number in these calculations to 1 s.f. and estimate the answers.
   a 73×38
   b $58 \div 17$
   c 324×67
   d 6.29^2
   e $\sqrt{97.2}$
   f $(42 + 58) \div 4.87$

14 🏠 Without using a calculator choose the correct answer, from the numbers given, to each of these calculations.
   a $53 \times 2.8 = 14.84,\ 1.484,\ 148.4$ **b** $7.2 \times 11.8 = 849.6,\ 84.96,\ 8.496$
   c $42.2 \times 35 = 1477,\ 14.77,\ 147.7$

Vertical sidebar text: 1 + 8 10,000 ÷ 2/3 × + 8 43 ÷ 1 10,000 × 1 4 9 16

USING PRIME FACTORS 9

1 Simplify these fractions by cancelling.

a $\frac{36}{45}$ b ✓ $\frac{56}{80}$ c $\frac{42}{49}$

d $\frac{14}{77}$ e $\frac{48}{66}$ f $\frac{54}{72}$

2 a Write 84 and 144 as a product of primes.
   b Find the HCF of 84 and 144.
   c Write $\frac{84}{144}$ in its lowest terms.

3 ✓ a Write 96 and 120 as a product of primes.
   b Find the HCF of 96 and 120.
   c Write $\frac{96}{120}$ in its lowest terms.

4 ✓ a Write 40 and 60 as a product of primes.
   b Find the LCM of 40 and 60.
   c Calculate $\frac{7}{40} + \frac{11}{60}$.

5 a Write 30 and 45 as a product of primes.
   b Find the LCM of 30 and 45.
   c Calculate $\frac{7}{30} + \frac{4}{45}$.

6 a Write 48 and 72 as a product of primes.
   b Find the LCM of 48 and 72.
   c Calculate $\frac{13}{48} - \frac{11}{72}$.

7 a Write 36 and 90 as a product of primes.
   b Find the LCM of 30 and 36.
   c Calculate $\frac{11}{36} - \frac{17}{90}$.

8 a ⬚ Write down a number, using two different digits, both less than 6, e.g. 34.
   b Reverse the digits to give a different number, e.g. 34 becomes 43.
   c Add the two numbers.
   d Repeat for other pairs of digits.
   e What do you notice about your answers? (Try to write at least two statements.)
   f Try to explain why these happen.

Consolidation Exercises

9 Simplify these fractions by cancelling.

a $\frac{27}{45}$ b $\frac{49}{63}$ c $\frac{84}{91}$ d $\frac{42}{56}$ e ✓ $\frac{45}{75}$ f $\frac{99}{132}$

10 🏠 Work out:

a $\frac{5}{12} + \frac{7}{18}$ b ✓ $\frac{5}{16} + \frac{13}{24}$ c $\frac{7}{24} + \frac{11}{36}$ d $\frac{11}{15} + \frac{13}{20}$ e $\frac{13}{16} - \frac{17}{40}$ f $\frac{23}{32} - \frac{29}{64}$

11 🔲 Extend question **8** to include digits greater than 5.

a In what ways are the results the same?

b How are they different?

c Explain why.

Challenging Exercises

12 a List all the common factors of $2x^2y$ and $6xy^2$.

b What is the HCF of $2x^2y$ and $6xy^2$?

13 Find the HCF of these pairs.

a mn^2 and m^2n b abc and a^2cd c $12pqr$ and $15p^2q$

d $4st^2$ and $2s^2t$ e x^3y^2 and x^2y^3 f $5uv^2w^2$ and $10u^2v^2w$

14 a Find the HCF of x^2y^5 and x^3y^4.   b Factorise $x^2y^5 + x^3y^4$.

15 Factorise these expressions:

a $24xy + 16yz$ b $3ab^2 + 6a^2b$ c $2(m + n) + 3(m + n)p$

16 🏠 Simplify these fractions by cancelling.

a $\dfrac{abc}{cde}$ b $\dfrac{x^2y^4}{x^3y}$ c $\dfrac{4r^3s}{6r^2s^3}$

10,000 ÷

2/3

×

+ 8

43

÷

1

10,000

×

1

4

9

16

ESTIMATING ROOTS

Essential Exercises

1 **a** Write down two consecutive integers which are nearest in value to $\sqrt{40}$.

   b Write down the square of the number halfway between your integers.

   c Use your judgement to decide whether 6.1 or 6.9 is nearer to $\sqrt{40}$.

   d Use your calculator to find the square of the number you decide is best.

   e Find $\sqrt{40}$ correct to 1 d.p. by squaring other numbers between 6.1 and 6.5.

2 The square root key on your calculator is broken. Without using the broken key find $\sqrt{68}$ correct to 2 d.p. Tabulate your working as shown below.

Trial	Number	Square	Comment
1	8	64	too small
2	9	_____	_____
3	8.5		
4	8.1		
5	8.2		
6	8.3		
7	8.25		
_____	_____		

3 Use the same broken calculator as in question **2** to work out these.

   a ✓ $\sqrt{32}$ **b** $\sqrt{75}$ **c** $\sqrt{97}$

4 A wooden cube has a volume of 10 cubic inches. The length of an edge can be worked out by finding the cube root of 10 ($\sqrt[3]{10}$). My calculator does not have a $\sqrt[3]{}$ key and so I will need to use a similar method to that used in question **2**. This is the beginning of my solution:

Trial	Number	Cube	Comment
1	2	$2^3 = 8$	too small
2	3	$3^3 =$ ____	_____
____	____		

Continue the solution to find the length of an edge correct to 2 d.p.

5 Find the difference between the two values of:

   a $\sqrt{64}$ **b** $\sqrt{81}$ **c** $\sqrt{400}$

6 Write down the value of:

   a $\sqrt[3]{-8}$ **b** $\sqrt[3]{-27}$ **c** $\sqrt[3]{-1000}$

7 Your calculator does not have a cube root ($\sqrt[3]{\ \ }$) key.

   Copy and continue the following table to find $\sqrt[3]{50}$ correct to 2 d.p.

Number	Cube	Comment
3	27	Too small
4		
3.5		
......		

8 Repeat question **7** to find the cube root of the following numbers.

   a ✓ 20   **b** 75   **c** 🏠 −5

   d How could you use a calculator to check your answers?

9 I think of a number and square it. When I add my number to its square the result is 23.37 correct to 2 d.p. Copy and continue the following table to find the number I thought of correct to 2 d.p.

Number x	x^2	$x^2 + x$	Comment
3	9	12	too small
4	16	20	too small
......			

10 🏠 Write down the value of:

   a $\sqrt[3]{-8000}$ **b** $\sqrt[3]{\dfrac{1}{27}}$ **c** $\sqrt[3]{0.125}$

Essential Exercises

1 Write down the value of these.

- **a** 30^3
- **b** 2^5
- **c** 11^0
- **d** 20^4
- **e** ✓ 10^{-2}
- **f** 1^6

2 Use the x^y key on your calculator to work out these.

- **a** 12^3
- **b** ✓ 7^5
- **c** 13^5
- **d** 8^4
- **e** 17^4
- **f** 28^3

3 By examining the last digits choose the correct answer from the three that are given.

- **a** $23^2 =$ 525   529   530
- **b** $32^3 =$ 32 768   32 770   32 766
- **c** $37^2 =$ 1365   1371   1369

4 True or false? Explain.

- **a** $\sqrt{7} + \sqrt{9} = \sqrt{16}$
- **b** $3^2 + 4^2 = 5^2$
- **c** $10^{-1} = -10$
- **d** $(-1)^6 = 1$

5 A bacterium divides once every twenty minutes. How many bacteria are there after two hours? Give your answer in index form and as an ordinary number.

6 Copy and complete the following:

$10^2 = \blacksquare$

$10^1 = \blacksquare$

$10^0 = \blacksquare$

$10^{-1} = \frac{1}{10} = \blacksquare$

$10^{-2} = \blacksquare = 0.01$

$10^{-3} = \blacksquare = \blacksquare$

$10^{-4} = \blacksquare = \blacksquare$

$10^{-5} = \blacksquare = \blacksquare.$

Consolidation Exercises

7 First estimate and then use a calculator to find, correct to 2 d.p.:
    a 2.1^4
    b ✓ 0.19^2
    c 1.87^5
    d 5.17^{-1}

8 Write down the value of:
    a 237.5×10^{-3}
    b 50.43×10^{-3}
    c ✓ $12\,300 \times 10^{-4}$

9 🏠 Write these as ordinary numbers.
    a 3.75×10^{-4}
    b 8.61×10^{-5}
    c 2.09×10^{-4}

10 Write these in standard form.
    a 0.53
    b 0.742
    c ✓ $0.040\,2$
    d $0.003\,7$
    e $0.000\,473$
    f $0.000\,075$

11 🧩 Without using a calculator work out the value of:
    a 11^2
    b 111^2
    c 1111^2
    d $11\,111^2$
    e What do you notice about your answers?
    f Predict the value of $111\,111^2$
    g Check your prediction by calculating $111\,111^2$

Challenging Exercises

12 🧩 **a** Using the results in question **11** predict the value of $11\,111\,111^2$.
    b Check your prediction by calculating $11\,111\,111^2$.
    c Will the pattern continue for $1\,111\,111\,111^2$.
       Why/Why not?

13 Write down the value of:
    a 2^{-1}
    b 2^{-2}
    c 2^{-3}
    d 3^{-1}
    e 7^{-1}
    f 5^{-2}

14 Find two equal pairs from the following.
    $\frac{1}{8}$, 3^{-2}, $\frac{1}{9}$, -8, 2^{-3}

15 🏠 Write down the value of:
    a $16^{\frac{1}{2}}$
    b $49^{\frac{1}{2}}$
    c $8^{\frac{1}{3}}$
    d $\frac{1}{2}^{-1}$

Index Laws 9

Essential Exercises

1 **a** Work out 2^3 and 2^4.

   b Multiply your answers.

   c Work out 2^7.

   d Explain the connection between the answers to **b** and **c**.

2 Write the answers to these in index form.

   a $2^2 \times 2^3$ **b** ✓ $2^2 \times 2^5$

   c $2^1 \times 2^4$ **d** $4^3 \times 4^2$

   e $5^2 \times 5^4$ **f** $3^3 \times 3^3$

3 **a** Work out 2^5 and 2^3.

   b Divide the first value by the second value.

   c Write your answer as a power of two.

   d What do you notice about the powers in **a** and your answers to **c**?

4 Write the answers to these in index form.

   a $3^4 \div 3^2$ **b** ✓ $10^5 \div 10^3$

   c $2^6 \div 2^2$ **d** $5^4 \div 5^3$

   e $4^5 \div 4^2$ **f** $3^6 \div 3^4$

Consolidation Exercises

5 Write the answers to these in index form.

   a $2^2 \times 2^3 \times 2^1$ **b** ✓ $3^3 \times 3^0 \times 3^4$

   c $10^2 \times 10^3 \times 10^4$ **d** $2^4 \times 2^3 \div 2^5$

   e $4^4 \div 4^2 \times 4^3$ **f** $5^2 \times 5^4 \div 5^3$

6 Calculate the value of these.

   a $7^4 \div 7^4$ **b** $2^6 \div 2^5$

   c $10^5 \div 10^3$ **d** $10^4 \times 10^5$

   e ✓ $1^6 \times 1^7$ **f** $2^3 \times 2^2$

7 a Write the answer to $2^3 \div 2^4$ in index form.

b Write down the equivalent division using ordinary numbers and give your answer as a fraction in its simplest form.

c Explain the connection between your answers.

8 🏠 Simplify these:

    a $a^2 \times a^4$ **b** $x^4 \times x^3$ **c** $p^2 \times p^3$

    d $y^4 \div y^2$ **e** $b^6 \div b^4$ **f** $w^5 \div w^2$

Challenging Exercises

9 a Work out $1.2 \times 10^3 \times 3.4 \times 10^4$ and give your answer in standard form.

    b What do you notice about the power of 10 in your answer.

    c Work out $4.3 \times 10^4 \times 2.9 \times 10^3$ and give your answer in standard form.

    d Does the same result happen in **c** as in **b**? Why\Why not?

10 Given that root $\sqrt{10}$ is approximately 3.2 find approximate values for:

    a $\sqrt{1000}$ **b** $\sqrt{100\,000}$ **c** $\sqrt{90}$

11 Find the value of:

    a $2^3 \times 2^3$ **b** $(2^3)^2$

    c $10^2 \times 10^2 \times 10^2$ **d** $(10^2)^3$

12 Write the answers to these in index form.

    a $(5^3)^2$ **b** $(3^3)^2$

    c $(4^2)^3$ **d** $(7^2)^3$

13 🏠 Simplify these:

    a $x^4 \times x^{-1}$ **b** $s^4 \times s^{-2}$ **c** $p^4 \div p^3$

    d $u^2 \div u^5$ **e** $(p^3)^2$ **f** $(y^2)^2$

    g $(s^4)^3$ **h** $(2y^2)^3$ **i** $(2t^3)^3$

14 Simplify these:

    a $a^p \times a^q$ **b** $c^m \div c^n$ **c** $x^a \times x^b \times x^c$ **d** $(u^2)^p$

EQUIVALENT FRACTIONS

Essential Exercises

1 Pentominoes are shapes made with five unit squares. Two examples are shown in the diagrams. (You may like to try to find all twelve possible shapes.)

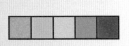

It is possible to fit all twelve pentominoes together to make a rectangle 6 squares by 10 squares.

What fraction of the rectangle would be covered by:

   a 3 pentominoes   **b** 7 pentominoes   **c** 11 pentominoes?

2 A pie chart shows the favourite colours of some children.

   a The orange sector has an angle of 150°.
      What fraction of the children preferred red?

   b If $\frac{2}{9}$ of the children preferred blue what is
      the angle for the blue sector?

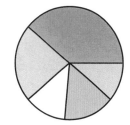

3 What fraction is the smaller quantity of the larger?

   a ✓ £96, £144   **b** 108 m, 90 m   **c** £2.10, 84p

   d 750 g, 2.5 kg   **e** 45 mm, 3.5 cm   **f** 2400 m, 1.6 km

4 What fraction is the larger quantity of the smaller?

   a 132, 88   **b** 240 g, 144 g   **c** 72 cm, 1.8 m

   d £6.40, 96p   **e** 4.8 km, 3600 m   **f** 3 gallons, 20 pints

5 What fraction is the first quantity of the second?

   a 225, 250   **b** ✓ 210 ml, 140 ml   **c** £360, £270

   d £1.32, 99p   **e** 180 mm, 7.5 cm   **f** 640 m, 1.6 km

6 These quantities are in imperial units.
What fraction is the first quantity of the second?

   a 10 ounces, $1\frac{1}{2}$ pounds   **b** 6 pints, 2 gallons

   c 8 inches, 1 foot 6 inches   **d** 2 feet, 15 inches

Consolidation Exercises

7 A small photograph 8 cm long and 5 cm wide is enlarged. The enlarged photograph is 20 cm long. How wide is it?

8 ✓ A scale drawing of a room is 30 cm long and 25 cm wide. If the room is 6 m long how wide is it?

9 🏠 Copy and complete the following:

a $\dfrac{m}{n} = \dfrac{5m}{\square}$

b $\dfrac{a}{b} = \dfrac{\square}{ab}$

c $\dfrac{u}{3w} = \dfrac{2uv}{\square}$

10 Simplify these by cancelling.

a $\dfrac{ax}{ay}$

b $\dfrac{3ab}{6bc}$

c $\dfrac{4s^2t}{2st}$

Challenging Exercises

11 A triangle of base 5 cm is enlarged to a triangle of base 10 cm. How many times larger is the area of the large triangle than the small triangle?

12 Simplify these by cancelling.

a $\dfrac{d^2ef}{de^2f}$

b $\dfrac{4a^2bc}{6ac^2}$

c $\dfrac{5x^4y^2}{10x^2y}$

d $\dfrac{3a + 6b}{3}$

e $\dfrac{4x^2 + 6x}{2x}$

f $\dfrac{rs + 2s}{s^2}$

13 🏠 Work out:

a $\dfrac{a}{2} + \dfrac{a}{3}$

b $\dfrac{2x}{3} + \dfrac{x}{5}$

c $\dfrac{u}{w} + \dfrac{v}{w}$

14 a Calculate $2\frac{3}{4} - 1\frac{1}{2}$

b Calculate $4\frac{5}{8} - 2\frac{3}{8}$

c What fraction is $(2\frac{3}{4} - 1\frac{1}{2})$ of $(4\frac{5}{8} - 2\frac{3}{8})$?

ORDERING FRACTIONS

Essential Exercises

1 Copy these and put > or < between them.

   a $\frac{1}{3}$ 0.3   **b** $\frac{5}{9}$ 0.6   **c** 0.7 $\frac{2}{3}$

   d 0.2 $\frac{1}{9}$ **e** ✓ $\frac{1}{2}$ $\frac{4}{9}$ **f** $\frac{8}{9}$ $\frac{3}{4}$

2 Which rectangle in each pair has the steepest diagonal?

   a

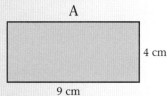 or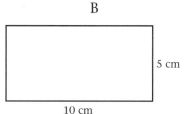

   b

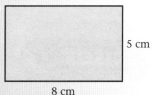 or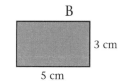

   c

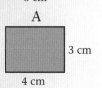 or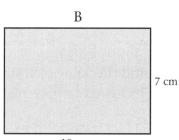

3 Write each list in order starting with the smallest.

   a ✓ $\frac{3}{10}, \frac{2}{5}, 0.\dot{3}$ **b** $\frac{5}{9}, \frac{1}{2}, 0.6$

4 In each of these sequences the terms increase by the same amount each time.
Find the amount of increase and then find the next term.

   a $\frac{1}{8}, \frac{3}{8}, \frac{5}{8}, \ldots$ **b** $\frac{3}{5}, 1\frac{1}{5}, 1\frac{4}{5}, \ldots$ **c** $\frac{1}{2}, \frac{7}{8}, \ldots$

   d $\frac{3}{5}, \frac{9}{10}, \ldots$ **e** $\frac{1}{5}, \frac{7}{15}, \ldots$ **f** $\frac{2}{3}, \frac{3}{4}, \ldots$

5 Find a fraction halfway between these pairs.

   a ✓ $0.\dot{3}$ and 0.5   **b** $0.\dot{6}$ and 0.75

Consolidation Exercises

6 Write these decimal numbers as improper fractions.

   a $1.\dot{2}$ **b** ✓ $3.\dot{5}$ **c** $2.\dot{7}$

7 🏠 In each of these sequences the terms increase or decrease by the same amount each time. Find the next term, in its simplest form.

   a $\frac{1}{3}, \frac{5}{6}, \ldots$ **b** $\frac{1}{2}, \frac{4}{5}, \ldots$ **c** $\frac{3}{4}, \frac{7}{12}, \ldots$

   d $\frac{14}{15}, \frac{2}{3}, \ldots$ **e** $1\frac{1}{2}, 1\frac{1}{5}, \ldots$ **f** $1\frac{7}{12}, 2\frac{1}{4}, \ldots$

8 Find a fraction half way between these pairs.

   a ✓ $0.\dot{2}$ and 0.5 **b** $0.\dot{3}$ and 0.4

9 Write each list in order starting with the smallest.

   a $\frac{1}{3}$, 0.3, $\frac{2}{5}$, $\frac{7}{20}$ **b** $\frac{7}{9}$, $\frac{2}{3}$, 0.6, $\frac{4}{5}$

Challenging Exercises

10 Show how to write these recurring decimals as fractions in their lowest terms.

   a $0.\dot{7}$ **b** $0.\dot{2}$

11 If $z = 0.\dot{2}\dot{7}$ find the value of $100z$. Combine these two statements to find a fraction in its lowest terms equal to $0.2727\ldots$

12 Change $0.\dot{6}\dot{3}$ to a fraction in its lowest terms.

13 🏠 Evaluate these if $a = 2$, $b = 3$, $c = 5$.

   a $\dfrac{(2a + 3b)}{4c}$ **b** $\dfrac{a}{b} + \dfrac{b}{c}$ **c** $\dfrac{a^2b}{c} + \dfrac{ab^2}{2c}$

14 Simplify these and then state which of each pair is greater if x and y are both greater than 1 and $x > y$.

   a $\dfrac{(12x + 9y)}{3}$ $\dfrac{(20x + 12y)}{4}$ **b** $\dfrac{(6x^2 + 8xy)}{2x}$ $\dfrac{(9xy + 12y)}{3y}$

   c $\dfrac{15x^2y}{5xy}$ $\dfrac{12xy}{4x}$ **d** $\dfrac{(6x^2 + 3y^2)}{3xy}$ $\dfrac{x}{y} + \dfrac{y}{x}$

ADDING AND SUBTRACTING FRACTIONS

Essential Exercises

1 Work out:

a $2\frac{3}{4} + \frac{5}{8}$ b $\frac{4}{5} + 3\frac{1}{2}$ c $1\frac{9}{10} + \frac{3}{5}$ d $\frac{7}{8} + 4\frac{1}{4}$

2 Work out:

a $2\frac{1}{3} + 1\frac{1}{2}$ b ✓ $1\frac{2}{5} + 3\frac{1}{3}$ c $1\frac{3}{7} + 6\frac{1}{2}$ d $5\frac{4}{5} + 3\frac{3}{10}$

3 Work out:

a $3\frac{3}{5} - 1\frac{1}{2}$ b ✓ $4\frac{6}{7} - 2\frac{3}{14}$ c $7\frac{3}{4} - 2\frac{2}{3}$ d $6\frac{7}{10} - 2\frac{2}{5}$

4 Work out:

a $\frac{7}{12} + \frac{5}{18}$ b $\frac{7}{15} + \frac{11}{20}$ c $\frac{9}{22} + \frac{27}{55}$ d $\frac{13}{15} + \frac{11}{30}$

5 Work out:

a $\frac{11}{12} - \frac{7}{18}$ b $\frac{11}{16} - \frac{7}{24}$ c $\frac{19}{21} - \frac{9}{14}$ d $\frac{11}{18} - \frac{8}{15}$

6 Jack spent $\frac{11}{24}$ of his homework time on Maths, $\frac{5}{16}$ on History and the remainder on French. What fraction of his homework time did he spend on French?

7 This table shows how long Meg spent on her homework each night last week.

Monday	$1\frac{1}{2}$ hours
Tuesday	$\frac{2}{3}$ hour
Wednesday	$\frac{3}{4}$ hour
Thursday	$1\frac{1}{12}$ hours
Friday	$2\frac{1}{3}$ hours

Calculate how long she spent on her homework last week.

Consolidation Exercises

8 Work out:

   a $6\frac{5}{8} + 2\frac{1}{2}$ **b** ✓ $3\frac{3}{4} + 1\frac{5}{8}$ **c** $4\frac{4}{5} + 2\frac{3}{10}$ **d** $5\frac{6}{7} + 4\frac{1}{2}$

9 Work out:

   a $3\frac{1}{2} - 1\frac{7}{8}$ **b** ✓ $4\frac{1}{4} - 2\frac{2}{3}$ **c** $2\frac{1}{5} - 1\frac{7}{10}$ **d** $4\frac{2}{9} - 1\frac{2}{3}$

10 🏠 Work out:

   a $3\frac{1}{8} + 1\frac{1}{4} + 2\frac{1}{2}$ **b** $2\frac{1}{2} + 3\frac{1}{3} + 1\frac{1}{6}$ **c** $6\frac{5}{6} + 2\frac{1}{3} + 4\frac{1}{2}$

11 🧩 There are some red, blue and green beads in a bag. The probability of selecting a red bead is $\frac{5}{21}$ and the probability of selecting a blue bead is $\frac{9}{14}$.

   a What is the probability of selecting a green bead?

   b What is the smallest possible number of beads in the bag?

Challenging Exercises

12 Work out:

   a $2\frac{3}{5} + 4\frac{7}{10} - 3\frac{2}{3}$ **b** $4\frac{2}{7} - 2\frac{1}{2} + 1\frac{11}{14}$ **c** $3\frac{2}{3} - 2\frac{3}{5} + \frac{11}{15}$

13 Three mixed numbers have a total of $7\frac{11}{12}$. Two of the numbers are $2\frac{3}{4}$ and $3\frac{2}{3}$. What is the third number, in its simplest form?

14 The difference between two mixed numbers is $1\frac{3}{5}$, the larger is $2\frac{2}{3}$, what is the smaller?

15 🏠 Simplify these expressions.

   a $\dfrac{1}{a} + \dfrac{1}{b}$ **b** $\dfrac{a}{b} + \dfrac{b}{a}$ **c** $\dfrac{3}{a} - \dfrac{2}{b}$ **d** $\dfrac{(a+b)}{2} - \dfrac{a}{3}$

16 Calculate:

   a $(4\frac{1}{3} + 2\frac{2}{5} - 1\frac{11}{15}) \times (2\frac{3}{8} - 1\frac{3}{4})$

   b $(2\frac{3}{14} + 1\frac{1}{2} - \frac{5}{7}) \times (\frac{1}{2} + \frac{5}{6})$

   c $(3\frac{5}{18} - 2\frac{1}{9} + 4\frac{5}{6}) \div (\frac{3}{4} - \frac{2}{3})$

FINDING A FRACTION OF A QUANTITY

9

Essential Exercises

1 Calculate:

   a $\frac{3}{8}$ of 22   **b** ✓ $\frac{7}{12}$ of 30   **c** $\frac{11}{15}$ of 180   **d** $\frac{19}{24}$ of 60

2 Use fractions to find:

   a 35% of 55   **b** $0.\dot{6}$ of 57   **c** ✓ 0.95 of 45   **d** 85% of 65

3 Calculate these to find which is greater in each pair.

   a $\frac{3}{8}$ of 32 or $\frac{2}{5}$ of 35   **b** $\frac{5}{7}$ of 42 or $\frac{2}{3}$ of 48

   c 45% of 22 or $\frac{4}{9}$ of 21   **d** $\frac{7}{8}$ of 92 or $\frac{8}{9}$ of 88

   e 74% of 125 or $\frac{7}{12}$ of 160   **f** 24% of 64 or $\frac{4}{5}$ of 24

4 Rita received £5.50 a week pocket money and Tom had £6.20. Rita saved $\frac{9}{25}$ of her pocket money and Tom saved $\frac{7}{20}$ of his. Who saved the most each week?

5 In a Maths test Jinit scored 19 out of 24 and in English he scored 13 out of 16. Which was the better score?

Consolidation Exercises

6 Mary received £4.80 pocket money each week. She spent $\frac{2}{5}$ of it on sweets and saved $\frac{5}{8}$ of the remainder. How much did she save each week?

Challenging Exercises

7 In a bag of mixed sweets $\frac{2}{5}$ were toffees, and $\frac{3}{10}$ were mints, and $\frac{3}{20}$ were fruit flavoured. The remaining six were jellies. What fraction of the sweets were jellies? How many sweets were in the bag?

9 MULTIPLYING FRACTIONS

Essential Exercises

1 Use cancelling to simplify these:

a $\frac{2}{3} \times \frac{6}{11}$ **b** ✓ $\frac{3}{5} \times \frac{4}{9}$ **c** $\frac{7}{10} \times \frac{5}{14}$ **d** $\frac{3}{4} \times \frac{10}{21}$ **e** $\frac{7}{8} \times \frac{2}{3}$

f $\frac{5}{6} \times \frac{3}{8}$ **g** $\frac{4}{5} \times \frac{7}{20}$ **h** $\frac{3}{7} \times \frac{7}{9}$ **i** $\frac{2}{3} \times \frac{9}{10}$

2 Copy and complete:

a $1\frac{1}{2} \times \frac{3}{4} = \frac{\blacksquare}{2} \times \frac{3}{4} = \frac{\blacksquare}{8} = 1\frac{\blacksquare}{8}$ **b** $2\frac{1}{3} \times 1\frac{1}{4} = \frac{\blacksquare}{3} \times \frac{\blacksquare}{4} = \frac{\blacksquare}{12} = 2\frac{\blacksquare}{12}$

c $2\frac{2}{3} \times 1\frac{3}{4} = \frac{\blacksquare}{3} \times \frac{\blacksquare}{4} = \frac{\blacksquare}{3} = 4\frac{\blacksquare}{3}$

3 Calculate:

a $1\frac{1}{3} \times \frac{2}{7}$ **b** ✓ $\frac{3}{4} \times 1\frac{4}{5}$ **c** $2\frac{1}{2} \times 1\frac{2}{5}$

4 Calculate the area of these rectangles.

a length $= \frac{4}{5}$ m, width $= \frac{3}{4}$ m   **b** length $= 1\frac{1}{2}$ yards, width $= \frac{3}{8}$ yard

Consolidation Exercises

5 Work out:

a $1\frac{2}{3} \times \frac{2}{5}$ **b** ✓ $\frac{5}{6} \times 1\frac{5}{7}$ **c** $3\frac{1}{2} \times 1\frac{1}{3}$

d $2\frac{1}{4} \times 1\frac{3}{5}$ **e** ✓ $2\frac{3}{8} \times 2\frac{2}{3}$ **f** $4\frac{3}{5} \times 3\frac{1}{3}$

6 🏠 Calculate:

a $\left(\frac{1}{2} + \frac{1}{3}\right) \times \frac{1}{4}$ **b** $\frac{3}{5} \times \frac{2}{9} + \frac{2}{3}$ **c** $\left(3 - 1\frac{3}{4}\right) \times \frac{4}{9}$

7 Calculate the area of a square of side $2\frac{1}{4}$ inches.

Challenging Exercises

8 Calculate:

a $\left(\frac{2}{3} + \frac{1}{5}\right) \times 2\frac{1}{2}$ **b** $\left(2\frac{2}{3}\right)^2$ **c** $\frac{2}{3} \times \frac{6}{7} \times \frac{5}{8}$ **d** $3\frac{1}{4} + \frac{2}{5} \times \frac{3}{8}$

9 🔲 **a** 🏠 Work out $\left(1 - \frac{1}{2}\right) \times \left(1 - \frac{1}{3}\right) \times \left(1 - \frac{1}{4}\right)$.

     b Work out $\left(1 - \frac{1}{2}\right) \times \left(1 - \frac{1}{3}\right) \times \left(1 - \frac{1}{4}\right) \times \left(1 - \frac{1}{5}\right) \times \left(1 - \frac{1}{6}\right)$.

     c Write down the answer when the list in **b** is extended to include $\times \left(1 - \frac{1}{10}\right)$.

DIVIDING FRACTIONS

Essential Exercises

1 **a** How many quarters are there in 1?   **b** How many quarters are there in 3?
   c Calculate $5 \div \frac{1}{4}$.

2 Find:
   a $\frac{1}{5} \times 4$ **b** $\frac{1}{5} \times 8$ **c** $\frac{2}{5} \times 3$

3 Work out:
   a $1 \div \frac{1}{8}$ **b** $2 \div \frac{1}{8}$ **c** $5 \div \frac{1}{8}$ **d** $\frac{1}{2} \div \frac{1}{8}$ **e** $\frac{1}{4} \div \frac{1}{8}$ **f** ✓ $\frac{3}{4} \div \frac{1}{8}$

4 **a** How many tenths are there in one half?   **b** Work out $\frac{1}{2} \div \frac{1}{6}$

5 Calculate:
   a $\frac{1}{2} \div \frac{1}{12}$ **b** $\frac{1}{3} \div \frac{1}{6}$ **c** $\frac{2}{3} \div \frac{1}{6}$ **d** $\frac{1}{5} \div \frac{1}{10}$ **e** $\frac{3}{5} \div \frac{1}{10}$ **f** ✓ $\frac{3}{5} \div \frac{3}{10}$

6 Calculate:
   a $\frac{2}{5} \div \frac{3}{10}$ **b** $\frac{4}{5} \div \frac{7}{10}$ **c** ✓ $\frac{7}{12} \div \frac{3}{4}$ **d** $\frac{2}{3} \div \frac{4}{5}$ **e** $\frac{5}{8} \div \frac{1}{4}$ **f** $\frac{7}{8} \div \frac{1}{2}$

Consolidation Exercises

7 Calculate:
   a $\frac{2}{3} \div \frac{2}{9}$ **b** $\frac{3}{4} \div \frac{2}{7}$ **c** ✓ $\frac{5}{6} \div \frac{2}{3}$ **d** $\frac{7}{8} \div \frac{2}{5}$
   e $\frac{9}{10} \div \frac{3}{4}$ **f** $\frac{11}{12} \div \frac{2}{9}$ **g** $2\frac{1}{2} \div \frac{3}{4}$ **h** $3\frac{1}{4} \div \frac{2}{5}$
   i ✓ $1\frac{7}{8} \div \frac{3}{5}$ **j** $4\frac{1}{2} \div \frac{2}{3}$ **k** $\frac{5}{8} \div 1\frac{1}{3}$ **l** $\frac{4}{7} \div 1\frac{3}{5}$

Challenging Exercises

8 🏠 Calculate:
   a $1\frac{2}{3} \div 1\frac{4}{5}$ **b** $2\frac{2}{3} \div 2\frac{2}{5}$ **c** $3\frac{1}{5} \div 1\frac{1}{3}$ **d** $4\frac{1}{3} \div 2\frac{3}{5}$
   e $2\frac{5}{6} \div 2\frac{1}{8}$ **f** $1\frac{1}{5} \div 3\frac{3}{7}$ **g** $(1 - \frac{2}{5}) \div (1 - \frac{3}{8})$ **h** $(\frac{3}{4} + \frac{2}{3}) \div 1\frac{3}{4}$

9 COMBINING FRACTIONS

1 Calculate:

a $\frac{5}{7} + \frac{1}{2}$

b ✓ $1\frac{3}{8} + \frac{1}{3}$

c $\frac{4}{5} - \frac{2}{3}$

d $\frac{2}{7} \times \frac{3}{5}$

e ✓ $\frac{5}{6} \div \frac{2}{3}$

f $\frac{9}{10} - \frac{1}{5}$

g $\frac{2}{3} - \frac{4}{9}$

h ✓ $2\frac{4}{5} - \frac{3}{4}$

i $\frac{8}{9} \times \frac{3}{4}$

j $1\frac{2}{3} + \frac{5}{6}$

k $(\frac{3}{4})^2$

l $\frac{5}{8} \div \frac{3}{5}$

m $2\frac{3}{4} + 1\frac{2}{3}$

n ✓ $1\frac{1}{2} \times \frac{3}{4}$

o $3 \div \frac{4}{5}$

p $3\frac{4}{9} - 1\frac{1}{3}$

q $\frac{11}{15} + \frac{7}{12}$

r $\frac{11}{20} \times \frac{15}{22}$

Consolidation Exercises

2 Calculate:

a $2\frac{2}{3} + 4\frac{5}{6}$

b $1\frac{1}{5} \div \frac{2}{3}$

c $5\frac{11}{12} - 3\frac{2}{3}$

d $2\frac{1}{2} \times \frac{4}{5}$

e $6\frac{5}{8} - 2\frac{3}{4}$

f $\frac{24}{35} \times \frac{15}{22}$

g $\frac{13}{36} + \frac{7}{24}$

h ✓ $2\frac{2}{5} \times 1\frac{3}{8}$

i $\frac{18}{25} \div \frac{11}{15}$

j $(3\frac{1}{3})^2$

k ✓ $1\frac{3}{4} \div 2\frac{4}{5}$

l $4\frac{2}{9} + \frac{5}{6} - 2\frac{1}{3}$

m $4\frac{3}{5} + 3\frac{1}{2} + 1\frac{7}{10}$

n $(1\frac{2}{3})^3$

Challenging Exercises

3 🏠 Calculate:

a $\frac{7}{18} + \frac{5}{12} - \frac{4}{9}$

b $\frac{4}{7} \times \frac{9}{16} \times \frac{14}{15}$

c $1\frac{3}{25} \div \frac{14}{75}$

d $1\frac{1}{2} \times 2\frac{1}{3} \times 3\frac{1}{4}$

e $\frac{3}{4} \times (2\frac{1}{2} - 1\frac{5}{6})$

f $(4\frac{2}{34} + 2\frac{5}{9}) \div (6\frac{1}{8} - 2\frac{1}{6})$

4 If $a = \frac{1}{2}$, $b = \frac{3}{4}$ and $c = \frac{5}{6}$ find the value of:

a abc

b $(a + b)c$

c ac^2

d $(b + c)^2$

e $c^2 \div b$

f $(a + b) \div (c - b)$

PERCENTAGE PROBLEMS

Essential Exercises

1 Find the selling price for each of these items.

	Item	Cost price	Profit
a	Computer	£840	15%
b ✓	Chair	£185	22%
c	CD	£12	16%
d	Radio	£35	35%

2 Find the profit or loss as a percentage of the cost price of these items.

	Item	Cost price	Selling price
a	Dress	£24	£31.20
b ✓	Anorak	£35	£44.80
c	Television	£480	£576.00

3 Which is the better buy?

a A packet of cereal weighing 750 g at a price of £1.25 or a special offer packet labelled '10% extra for only 10p extra'. Explain your answer.

b A large (200 g) jar of coffee with 20% extra at £4.50 or two standard (100 g) jars at £1.85 each?

4 The price paid for these meals included a service charge of 10%. What was the price before the service charge was added?

a Sausage, beans and chips for £3.30

b Cheese omelette for £4.95

c Roast beef dinner for £7.15

5 The following table shows some salary increases. Find the missing values.

Salary	% increase	New salary
£8500	6%	_____
£12 600	5%	_____
£20 000	_____	£20 800
£5250	_____	£5355

Consolidation Exercises

6 This table shows information about price reductions in a sale. Calculate the missing values.

	Original price	% Reduction	Sale price
a	£60	15%	_____
b ✓	£48	_____	£42
c	£16	_____	£12.80
d	_____	10%	£ 7.20
e	_____	25%	£24
f	_____	30%	£38.50

7 Which is the better buy, five pairs of socks for the usual price, £10, of a four-pair pack, or a price reduction of 25% on a pack of four pairs? Explain.

8 The population of the world is about 6200 million. It is estimated that about 27% of people speak English and 19% speak Chinese. Find, correct to one decimal place, how many million people speak English and how many million speak Chinese.

9 A photograph is enlarged by 10%. What is the percentage increase in its area?

10 a A school increased the length of its day by 5%. The original length was 4 hours 50 minutes. What is the length of the new day, correct to the nearest minute?
   b A company decreased its working week by 5%. How long is the new working week if the original length was 40 hours.

11 Mrs Bennett pays 10% income tax on £3100 of her earnings and 22% tax on the remaining £9600. How much tax does she pay altogether?

12 Mrs Summers pays £12 000 for her new car. During the first year it loses 40% of its value and in the second year it depreciates by a further 30%.
 a What is the value of the car at the end of the first year?
 b What is its value after two years?
 c What percentage of its value is lost in two years?

13 When water freezes to ice the volume increases by 4%. How much water will be produced when a two-litre block of ice melts?

14 Find the value of these investments when compound interest has been added.

	Investment	Rate of interest	Time invested
a	£1000	5%	2 years
b	£2500	4%	3 years
c	£6200	7%	5 years

15 A shopkeeper bought 500 postcards for £25 and sold them in packs of ten at a profit of 28% per pack. At the end of the year he still had twelve packs left and decided to reduce the price by 50% in a sale. If he sold all the cards in the sale did he make a loss or profit on his original purchase? How much? Calculate what percentage this is of the original cost, correct to 1 d.p.

16 A tree of height 120 cm was planted. It grew by 30% in the first year, 25% in the second year and 20% in the third year. How tall was it after 3 years?

17 A carpet fitter over-estimates lengths by 5%. A room measures 480 cm by 550 cm.
 a Calculate the carpet fitter's estimate of the area.
 b By what percentage does he over-estimate the area. (Give your answer to 2 decimal places.)

USING DIRECT PROPORTION

Essential Exercises

1 The ingredients for making 75 pieces of chocolate fudge include 450 g sugar, 25 g butter, 150 ml water and 100 g chocolate.

  a ✓ How much sugar would be needed to make 90 pieces of fudge?

  b Alison has 240 g chocolate for making fudge. How much butter will she need to mix with it? How many pieces of fudge will this make?

  c Sam and David plan to make 600 pieces of fudge to sell at a charity stall. How much sugar, butter, chocolate and water will they need?

  d It takes Sam and David two hours to make half the fudge so they decide to invite six friends to help make the rest on the following evening. How long do you think it will take them all? Explain your answer.

2 It takes three men three hours to paint a room.

  a ✓ How long would it take one man to paint the same room?

  b How long would it take 30 men?

3 A gardener can plant fifteen rose bushes in two hours.

  a How long would it take him to plant 50 bushes if he worked at the same rate?

  b How many rose bushes could he plant in one hour twenty minutes?

  c If he started work at 7 a.m. and finished at 7 p.m. could he plant 90 bushes? Explain your answer.

4 It takes Mrs Grey 2 hours 40 minutes to groom 8 horses.

  a How long does it take her to groom 13 horses?

  b How many horses can she groom in 1 hour 40 minutes?

5 A set of 35 maths textbooks takes up 56 cm of shelf space.

  a How much shelf space is needed for 100 books?

  b How many books would fill 104 cm of shelf space?

1 + 8 10,000 ÷ 2/3 × + 8 43 ÷ 1 10,000 × 1 4 9 16

Consolidation Exercises

6 At constant speed the distance travelled is proportional to the time taken.

  a Ahmed walks 9 km in $1\frac{1}{2}$ hours. How long does it take him to walk 7 km at the same speed?

  b ✓ It takes Jenny $\frac{1}{4}$ hour to cycle 5 km. How far does she cycle in 24 minutes at the same speed?

7 🏠 The mass of a solid block is proportional to its volume. Work out these masses and volumes.

  a If 20 cm³ of wax has a mass of 16 g find the mass of 55cm³.

  b If a 40 g block of steel has a volume of 5 cm³ find the volume of a 72 g block.

  c If 0.5 g of polystyrene has a volume of 50 cm³ find the mass of 210 cm³.

  d If 8 cm³ of gold has a mass of 152 g find the volume of a 209 g block.

Challenging Exercises

8 If y is proportional to x and $y = 21$ when $x = 7$ find:

  a the value of y when $x = 4$

  b the value of x when $y = 27$

9 If $p \propto q$ and $p = 3$ when $q = 12$ find:

  a the value of p when $q = 22$

  b the value of q when $p = 7$

10 🏠 If $A \propto l^2$ and $A = 80$ when $l = 4$ find:

  a A when $l = 8$

  b l when A = 500

11 d varies directly with t, and $d = 105$ when $t = 3$.

  a Find d when $t = 5$

  b Find t when $d = 280$

  c What would the letters d and t represent?

  d In this case, what is represented by the constant of proportionality?

Essential Exercises

1 Write these ratios in whole-number form.

a $\frac{1}{3} : 4$

b $3 : \frac{1}{5}$

c $\frac{2}{5} : \frac{3}{5}$

d $\frac{1}{2} : \frac{1}{3}$

e ✓ $\frac{1}{2} : \frac{3}{4}$

f $\frac{2}{3} : \frac{1}{6}$

g $\frac{3}{10} : \frac{4}{5}$

h $1\frac{1}{2} : 5$

i $2 : 2\frac{1}{4}$

j $1\frac{1}{2} : 3\frac{1}{2}$

k ✓ $1\frac{1}{4} : 1\frac{3}{4}$

l $1\frac{1}{2} : 1\frac{3}{4}$

m $0.3 : 1$

n $2 : 0.7$

o $1.4 : 2.1$

2 Change these ratios to the form $1 : m$.

a $2 : 6$

b ✓ $5 : 20$

c $12 : 60$

d $\frac{1}{4} : 1$

e $0.1 : 1$

f $0.2 : 0.8$

3 Change these ratios to the form $m : 1$.

a $12 : 4$

b $21 : 7$

c $45 : 5$

d $1 : \frac{1}{3}$

e ✓ $1 : 0.5$

f $1.2 : 0.3$

Consolidation Exercises

4 Write these ratios in whole number form.

a $1 : \frac{3}{4}$

b $1 : 2\frac{1}{8}$

c $1 : 3.7$

d $\frac{7}{9} : 1$

e $3\frac{3}{4} : 1$

f $0.83 : 1$

5 Write these ratios in simplified whole-number form.

a $\frac{3}{4} : 1\frac{1}{2}$

b $1\frac{1}{5} : 1\frac{4}{5}$

c $2\frac{2}{3} : 3\frac{1}{3}$

6 Change these ratios to the form $1 : m$.

a $2 : 5$

b $8 : 10$

c $10 : 35$

7 Change these ratios to the form $m : 1$.

a $7 : 2$

b $9 : 4$

c $27 : 10$

8 🔲 🏠 This table shows the ratio of weights of flour and fat for some pastries.

Pastry	Flour : fat
Flaky	8 : 5
Choux	3 : 1
Chocolate	8 : 3½
Shortcrust	2 : 1
Rich cheese	4 : 4½ (including cheese)
Puff	8 : 7
Suet crust	8 : 3

a Which pastry, shortcrust or choux, has the lower proportion of fat? Explain.

b Which pastry, suet crust or chocolate, has the higher proportion of fat? Explain.

c Which pastry has twice as much fat in proportion to flour as chocolate pastry? Explain.

Challenging Exercises

9 🔲 🏠 Mr Blake is advised by his doctor to go on a low fat diet.

a Convert each of the ratios in the table in question **8** to the form $1 : m$.

b Which pastry should Mr Blake avoid?

c Which pastry would you advise him to choose?

10 🔲 A model car is made to a scale of 1 : 43. If the model is 8.2 cm calculate the length of the real car in metres correct to 2 decimal places.

11 🔲 This table shows the scales of three different plans of the same school.

Plan A	1 : 20
Plan B	2 cm to 1 m
Plan C	0.1 : 1

Which plan uses the largest sheet of paper? Explain your answer.

USING RATIOS

1 On a large plate of sandwiches the ratio of the numbers of ham, cheese and egg sandwiches is 2 : 3 : 4. If there are 72 sandwiches how many of each type are there? Remember to check your answers.

2 Use the information about the proportions of flour and fat in different pastries (in the table on page 107) to answer these questions.

   a To make 20 choux buns you need 220 g of choux pastry. How much flour is needed?

   b Mrs Young makes three large flans for a party. For each flan she needs 350 g shortcrust pastry. How much fat will she need?

   c Sausage rolls are made with 260 g flaky pastry. How much flour is needed?

3 This table shows the proportions of protein, fat and carbohydrates in various foods.

Food	Protein	:	Fat	:	Carbohydrate
Ice cream	4	:	12	:	20
Tomatoes	0.8	:	0	:	2.4
Strawberries	0.6	:	0	:	6
Cheese	25	:	35	:	0
Chips	4	:	9	:	37
Fruit yoghurt	4.8	:	1	:	18.2
Wholemeal bread	10	:	3	:	47

   a ✓ Write down and simplify the ratio of protein to fat in cheese.

   b How much protein is there in 240 g of cheese?

   c How much carbohydrate is there in one tomato weighing 48 g?

   d How much protein is there in 220 g strawberries?

   e How much protein is there in three 36 ml scoops of ice cream?

4 An old map of Lincolnshire uses a scale of 1 inch to 5 miles.

    a The distance from Lincoln to Skegness by road is 44 miles. How far is this on the map?

    b ✓ The distance from Grantham to Woolsthorpe Manor (the birthplace of Sir Isaac Newton) is 1.4 inches on the map. How far did Isaac Newton travel to school in Grantham?

    c The distance between Gainsborough and Lincoln measures 5.2 inches on the map. How far does the air ambulance fly to take a patient from Gainsborough to Lincoln Hospital?

5   **a** On average the height of a boy increases by 20% between the ages of ten and sixteen. Find the ratio of the height of a ten-year-old boy to the height of a sixteen-year-old boy.

    b On average the weight of a girl increases by 60% between the ages of ten and sixteen. Find the ratio of the weight of a ten-year-old girl to the weight of a sixteen-year-old girl.

6 Use information in the table in question **3** to answer these questions.

    a How much protein is there in 125 g of fruit yoghurt?

    b How much fat is there in a 150 g portion of chips?

    c What fraction of a loaf of wholemeal bread is protein?

7 🏠 The table below shows some of the nutrition information provided on a pot of fruit yoghurt.

    a Write the ratio 125 : 100 in the form 1 : n and n : 1.

    b Use the appropriate form to calculate the missing values.

Typical values	per 125 g pot	per 100 g
Energy	124 kcal	_____
Protein	_____	4.8 g
Carbohydrate	19.8 g	_____
Fat	_____	1.8 g

8 ✓ A model car is made to a scale of 1 : 50.

    a If the car is 3.6 m long how long is the model?

    b The model is 3.8 cm wide how wide is the car?

    c What is the ratio of the number of windows on the model to the number of windows on the car.

Challenging Exercises

Areas and volumes of enlargements

9 The table shows the length, width and scale factor of enlargement of four rectangles.

Rectangle	Length	Width	Scale factor of enlargement
A	11 cm	8 cm	2
B	2.2 cm	5 cm	5
C	3.4 cm	7.2 cm	10
D	14 cm	6 cm	0.5

  a For each rectangle write down the ratio of the length of the original rectangle to the length of the enlarged rectangle.

  b Calculate the area of the original and the enlarged rectangles.

  c For each rectangle work out the ratio of the area of the original rectangle to the area of the enlarged rectangle. Give your answers in the form $1 : n$.

  d Compare your answers to **a** and **c**. Describe any patterns.

10 A cuboid with length 9 cm, width 7 cm and height 3 cm is enlarged by a scale factor of two.

  a Find the volume of the original cuboid and the volume of the enlarged cuboid.

  b Find the ratio of the volume of the original cuboid to the volume of the enlarged cuboid. Give your answer in its simplest form.

  c Suggest a possible connection between the ratio of the lengths in each cuboid and the ratio of volumes.

  d Test your suggestion by enlarging some more cuboids by different scale factors. (A spreadsheet could be helpful.)

  e If your suggestion was correct explain why it works.

11 A boat is 6 m long. A model of the boat is 30 cm long.

  a Find the scale used to make the model in the form $1 : n$.

  b If the boat is 1.8 m wide how wide is the model in cm?

  c If the model has 2 sails find the number of sails on the boat.

  d If the deck area of the model is 190 cm² find the deck area of the boat in m².

  e If the stowage capacity on the model is 90 cm³ find the stowage capacity on the boat in m³.

ANSWERS TO SELF-CHECK QUESTIONS

YEAR 7

Place value in integers
6c 140 000 **g** 4000
7c seven hundred thousand 700 000
15b 2 480 000 **d** 60 600

Place value in decimals
3b 405 **d** 0.24
5d five hundredths
9b 10.82 **10b** 7.519 **11c** 2.371

Written calculations
1a 2914 **2a** 2483 **3a** 6494
4a 53

Ordering decimals
3b 34 mm **6b** 3.24 g, 3.3 g, 3.39 g
25b 7.238 **26a** 0.25 m **b** 21 mm

Rounding integers
2a 2 kg **b** 1900 g **c** 1880 g
6a 225 **b** 234
12a $20 \times 70 = 1400$

Rounding decimals
4a 63 m **b** 63.0 m
7c 4 **8c** 7.1 **13a** 6, 3

Negative numbers
4b -4 **c** -5
5b $+5$ **14a** $+2$ **18a** 0
23 Ann's height is 132 ± 0.5 cm

Multiples, factors and prime numbers
4a 54, 63, 72, 81, 90, 99
7b 1, 2, 4, 7, 14, 28
11a 2, 4, 6, 8, 10, 12, 14, 16, 18, 20;
5, 10, 15, 20; LCM = 10
13a 1, 2, 5, 10; 1, 3, 5, 15; HCF = 5
20b 40 **21b** 18

Some special numbers
6b 7 **8** $9 + 16 = 25$
12a 400 **14a** 5.5

Fractions
7a $\frac{5}{8}$ **9c** 6 **10c** 21 **11c** 2
12c $\frac{1}{4}$ **16a** 23 **17c** $\frac{11}{4}$ **20b** $5\frac{1}{2}$
25b $\frac{1}{3}$ **f** $\frac{1}{10}$ **27b** $\frac{2}{5}$ **29a** $7\frac{1}{3}$
30a $\frac{27}{4}$

Fractions and decimals
1c $\frac{1}{5}$ **6c** $\frac{9}{20}$ **9a** 0.4 **10b** $6\frac{1}{5}$
14a 2.1, $2\frac{3}{10}$, $2\frac{1}{2}$, 2.6
15b $0.25 < \frac{1}{3}$ **16b** $\frac{3}{4} > \frac{7}{10}$
19a $2\frac{1}{10}$ **20a** $4\frac{4}{5}$ **21a** 7.1
23b $0.51 > \frac{1}{2}$

Adding and subtracting fractions
4c $\frac{2}{3}$ **5b** $1\frac{3}{8}$ **6d** $\frac{1}{3}$
10c 1 **11e** $\frac{5}{8}$

Fractions and integers
3c 12 **7c** $3\frac{1}{3}$
10c £27 **11c** 700 g
15a $\frac{15}{2}$ (= $7\frac{1}{2}$, the rest are all 3)

Percentage, fraction, decimal equivalents
2c $\frac{4}{5}$ **4b** $1\frac{1}{5}$ **6c** $\frac{30}{100}$, 30% **7b** 0.4
13c $\frac{35}{100}$, 35% **14b** 85%

Finding a percentage of ...
1b £90
4a 8 cm **b** 4 cm **c** 12 cm
8a 4 m **b** 12 m **c** 32 m
19a £700 **b** 7 **c** £693

Percentages with a calculator
1b 3.36 **3b** £14.72
8a $\frac{1}{2}$ of £80 = £40 **b** £41.31

Ratio and proportion
3a 36 servings **b** 4 packets
7c 2 : 3 **8b** £10
12 40 ounces **14** 2 days

YEAR 8

Powers of ten
5b 4 **7d** 0.03 **9b** 41
18c 5365 **19b** 8.991 **21b** 0.07

Ordering decimals
3c $3.841 > 3.814$ **5d** 2.765
10 0.65201, 0.6502, 0.6250, 0.6205, 0.0652

Rounding
2 70 000 km^2
8 France 58.81 millions, Germany 82.08 millions
10a 72.96 **b** 73.0 **c** 73
13 a 551 500 km^2

Positive and negative integers (adding and subtracting)
1h 1 **m** -12 **r** 11 **4c** 0
7c 3 **j** -18

Positive and negative integers (multiplying and dividing)
2c -16 **g** 30 **5c** 3
7c -4 **8c** -7
9b -54 **f** 6

Multiples and factors
3c $3 \times 5 \times 5$ **4b** 4 **5b** 220
8b 18 **9b** 110

Powers and roots
2a 1, 25, 64, 81 **b** 1, 8, 27, 64
c 1, 64 **9a** 32 **11a** 2.83
15a $\sqrt{25} < \sqrt{30} < \sqrt{36}$ 5, 6

Comparing fractions and decimals
1c $\frac{27}{40}$ **2c** 3.8 **4c** 0.53
6a $\frac{7}{10}, \frac{3}{4}, \frac{4}{5}$
12c $0.7\dot{7}$, 0.78 **e** $2.\dot{3}$, 2.33

Adding and subtracting fractions
3b $\frac{19}{24}$ **4j** $1\frac{11}{18}$ **6f** $\frac{1}{12}$
10e $3\frac{7}{10}$ **11b** $4\frac{3}{10}$

Multiplying and dividing integers and fractions
1b $\frac{4}{5}$ **2c** £67.50 **4b** $9\frac{1}{3}$
11b $18\frac{2}{3}$ **12f** 12

Converting fractions, decimals and percentages
1b $\frac{8}{25}$ **2c** 82%
3c 54.5% **4b** 70%
10b $3\frac{1}{2}$ **12b** 209%

Working with percentages
2b 9.1 **4b** 1.89
12b 4.32 g **13b** £237.51

Percentage change
2b 72 **3b** 110.76 kg
4c £11.20
7b 359.04 **8b** £104.58

Using direct proportion
2 42p **6a** 6 eggs
9a 6 cm wide, 24 cm long **b** 10 m

Simplifying ratios
2c 4 **3b** 1 : 4 **h** 10 : 3
8b $\frac{7}{10}$ **9e** 3 : 4 : 5

Dividing in a given ratio
2 £12, £16 **5** 9 granddaughters
8 25 pupils

YEAR 9

Using powers of ten

1c 0.0065 **g** 19.4

3b 70 **4c** $\frac{2}{5}$, 0.4

6b 1.2 cm^3

Standard form

2b 5.64 **f** 64.3 **3a** 6300 **4a** 3

10b 0.0138 **11a** 8.64×10^3

Rounding

1b 2 **2b** 4.0 **3b** 1.64

7b 0.06 **8b** 62 000 **9b** 53.9

Estimating

1b 54 **f** 36 **3a** 17.1 m^2

7 7500

Using prime factors

1b $\frac{7}{10}$

3a $96 = 2 \times 2 \times 2 \times 2 \times 2 \times 3$,
$120 = 2 \times 2 \times 2 \times 3 \times 5$

b 24 **c** $\frac{4}{5}$

4a $40 = 2 \times 2 \times 2 \times 5$,
$60 = 2 \times 2 \times 3 \times 5$

b 120 **c** $\frac{43}{120}$

9e $\frac{3}{5}$ **10b** $\frac{41}{48}$

Estimating roots

3a 5.66

8a 2.71

Indices

1e $\frac{1}{100}$ (0.01) **2b** 16 807

7b 0.04, 0.04

8c 1.23 **10c** 4.02×10^{-2}

Index laws

2b 2^7 **4b** 10^2

5b 3^7 **6e** 1

Equivalent fractions

3a $\frac{2}{3}$ **5b** $\frac{3}{2}$ ($1\frac{1}{2}$)

8 5 m

Ordering fractions

1e $\frac{1}{2} > \frac{4}{9}$ **3a** $\frac{3}{10}, 0.3, \frac{2}{5}$ **5a** $\frac{5}{12}$

6b $\frac{32}{9}$ **8a** $\frac{13}{36}$

Adding and subtracting fractions

2b $4\frac{11}{15}$ **3b** $2\frac{9}{14}$

8b $5\frac{3}{8}$ **9b** $1\frac{7}{12}$

Finding a fraction of a quantity

1b $17\frac{1}{2}$ **2c** $42\frac{3}{4}$

Multiplying fractions

1b $\frac{4}{15}$ **3b** $1\frac{7}{20}$

5b $1\frac{3}{7}$ **e** $6\frac{1}{3}$

Dividing fractions

3f 6 **5f** 2 **6c** $\frac{7}{9}$

7c $1\frac{1}{4}$ **i** $3\frac{1}{8}$

Combining fractions

1b $1\frac{17}{24}$ **e** $1\frac{1}{4}$ **h** $2\frac{1}{20}$ **n** $1\frac{1}{8}$

2h $3\frac{3}{10}$ **k** $\frac{5}{8}$

Percentage problems

1b £225.70 **2b** 28%

6b 12.5%

Using direct proportion

1a 540 g **2a** 9 hours

6b 8 km

Simplifying and comparing ratios

1e 2 : 3 **k** 5 : 7

2b 1 : 4 **3e** 2 : 1

Using ratios

3a 5 : 7

4b 7 miles

8a 7.2 cm **b** 1.9 m **c** 1 : 1